Orchid Ayurvedic Creations
by Adhiраже Luна

May You Learn by Meditation Cards
Seven (Sīменал) Edít

Other Intentional Creations
by Adrienne Enns

May You Know Joy Meditation Cards
Seeds of Intention Cards

INTENTIONAL DAYS
CREATING YOUR LIFE ON PURPOSE

INTENTIONAL DAYS

CREATING YOUR LIFE ON PURPOSE

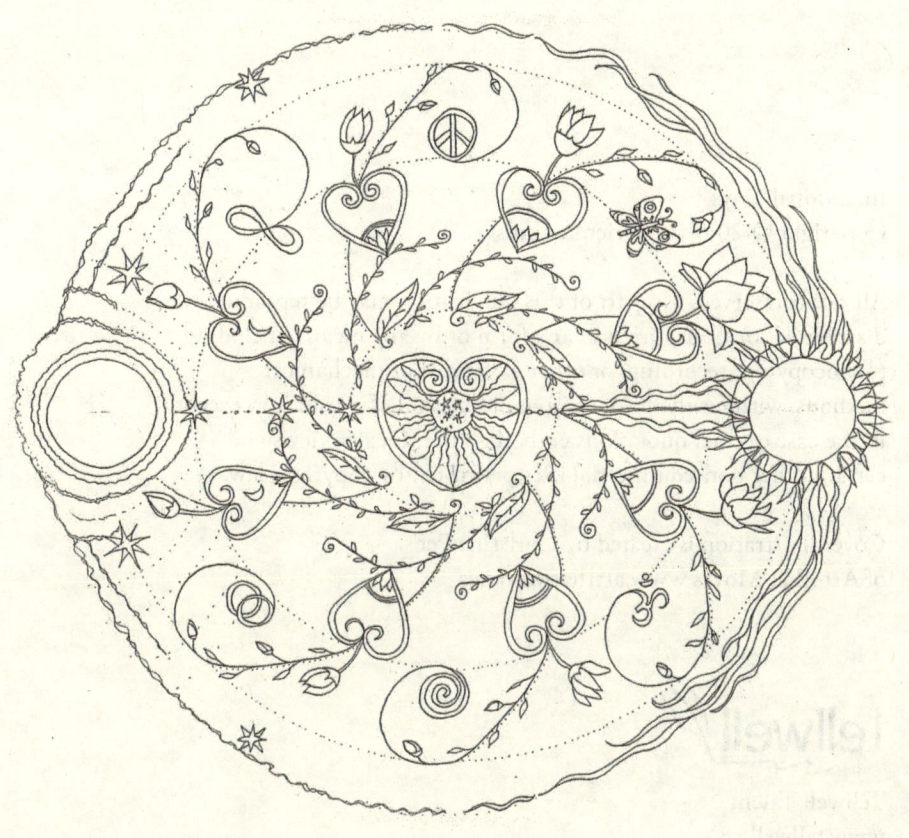

ADRIENNE ENNS

Intentional Days
Copyright © 2019 by Adrienne Enns

All rights reserved. No part of this publication may be reproduced, distributed, or transmitted in any form or by any means, including photocopying, recording, or other electronic or mechanical methods, without the prior written permission of the author, except in the case of brief quotations embodied in critical reviews and certain other non-commercial uses permitted by copyright law.

Cover illustration is created by Christine Pensa
of Art That Moves www.artthatmoves.ca

Tellwell Talent
www.tellwell.ca

ISBN
978-0-2288-1506-8 (Paperback)
978-0-2288-1507-5 (eBook)

For Maddie & Jack

You are my seeds of inspiration—flourishing every day.
May you know great joy & infinite adventures.

Enneirda Morris Steinberg sends her love.

Tell me, what is it you plan to do with your one wild and precious life?
Mary Oliver

*Out beyond ideas of wrongdoing and rightdoing
there is a field. I'll meet you there.
When the soul lies down in that grass, the world is too full to talk about.*
Rumi

*Don't call it uncertainty—call it wonder.
Don't call it insecurity—call it freedom.*
Osho

Intentional Days Mantra

I have deep reverence for my moments.
I know that moments turn into days
turn into weeks turn into years.

I know that my greatest joy,
my deepest truth
and my highest sense of purpose
are already within me.
I honor them.
I see them.
I feel them.
I will know them, embody them
and live them.

I will show up in this world
as the fullest expression of myself.
I will be wise and knowing.
I will be curious.
I will be open.
I will enjoy
and I will celebrate.

I will be kind to myself.
I will love myself deeply.
I will choose to nourish
everything that connects me
with my highest self.
I will allow the radiance of this energy
to extend to the people and the world around me.

I remind myself that all of my intentional days
create a life on purpose.

The light in me honors the light in you.
Namaste.

TABLE OF CONTENTS

Prologue xxiii

Intentional Living 1
Creating Our Lives on Purpose 29
My Daily Intentions 45
    Abundance 49
    Activism 51
    Awareness 53
    Being 55
    Beauty 57
    Beyond Fear 59
    Bless This, Too 61
    Bring the Sass 63
    Choice 65
    Commitment 67
    Connection 69
    Courage 71
    Curiosity 73
    Defying Logic 75
    Embodiment 77
    Enough 79
    Forgiveness 81
    Freedom 83
    Gratitude 85

Growth	87
Honoring My Feelings	89
Hope	91
I Am a Creator	93
I Am Worthy	95
I Savor	97
In the Flow	99
Infinite Possibilities	101
Kindness	103
Knowing	105
Life is Rigged in My Favor	107
Love	109
Love vs. Fear	111
Magic	113
Me, Myself and I	115
Me & Time	117
My Adventures	119
My Breath	121
My Deepest Joy	123
My Greatness	125
My Heart	127
My Highest Self	129
My Wild Spirit	131
Navigating Change	133
On Tough Days	135
Open	137
Perfectly Imperfect	139
Pressing Pause	141
Purpose	143
Release	145
Reverence & Grace	147
Showing Up	149
So Much to Celebrate	151
The Next Right Thing	153
This Moment	155

Truth	157
Uncertainty	159
What If?	161
Willing to Fail	163
Wholeness	165
With Gratitude	169
About Adrienne	171

Dear Reader,

I'm grateful that our paths have crossed and don't imagine it's a coincidence. You are meant to weave greater intention into your own life in beautiful and meaningful ways. Use this as a guidebook, remembering that you are the creator in your own life. Intention setting is a simple yet powerful practice you can make uniquely your own.

This practice of being intentional is something I discovered for myself. It didn't come with a name or directions. I was beginning again and wanted to create a new life that nourished and inspired me. As I stood on the brink of the rest of my life, I knew three things: (1) Instead of being defined by my worst moments, I would use them as a catalyst for change; (2) I wanted to show up authentically and create my life on purpose; (3) If I was going to go to all the trouble to turn my life around, I wanted to be deeply joyful. Every. Damn. Day.

At this critical moment in my life, I paused and asked myself *What am I putting my energy into? What if I put all that energy into living a life I really loved?* This was the seed of my own intentional living. Up until that point, I'd successfully dug a deep hole for myself. Imagine what I could do if I wielded the power of my thoughts, feelings and actions for good? What would daily joyful living actually look and feel like? What inspiration did I want to fuel me? What was I really committing myself to?

These lessons have been my greatest gifts and it is a pleasure to share them with you. We all have raw material in our lives and it's what we choose to do with it that really matters. This is what it means to be intentional. I hope that you will feel inspired and empowered to integrate an intention practice into your everyday.

In this book, you will learn what being intentional means and why it's worth it. I will provide you with simple and practical ways to layer intention into your moments, days and even years. Finally, I've created a whole new series of raw and beautiful intentions with affirmations. I hope you love reading them as much as I enjoyed writing them. You can read this book front to back or, as I recommend, pick it up daily to find just what you need to navigate your course. My intention is that it finds a special place in your days and in your heart.

It's only fair to warn you that embracing this way of living is not for the faint of heart. To live intentionally is to fully participate in life. It's game on and we're not heckling from the cheap seats, we're on the field. It's intense, exhilarating and the gifts that come meeting life this way are unparalleled. I hope you're ready. Let's know what it feels like to be wildly alive.

I believe that My Highest Self, (The Universe, This Divine Creator, God or whichever identifier resonates with you) wants us to be happy and to grow. I think he or she has a marvelous sense of humor. I think they want us to get over ourselves, show up and love each other. I think they want us to celebrate life, not struggle with it. I think they are always supporting us, and all our experiences are opportunities to grow. I believe the only way to truly thrive and revere this human experience is to fully engage with it, live into it and through it.

As I write this to you, it's early spring in Toronto. Ice is melting and hope in the form of buds and crocuses is popping. Spring reminds me of how being intentional has blossomed in my own life. The seeds of my life today and of this book were planted many years ago. They've been fertilized, watered and nurtured. They've also endured many harsh winters. Intentional growth can take time, but like any perennial garden, it matures, flourishes and becomes more robust with each season. The book you hold in your hands feels, to me, like a gorgeous bloom after many seasons.

Each moment is an opportunity and so is each day. I honor my whole journey because it delivered me here and I believe the seeds of this lifetime were planted a long time ago. All this to say: the days add up. They keep me alive and thriving. Intentional days create a life on purpose.

Thank you for joining me on this journey. I wish you incredible moments, amazing adventures and deep joy always.

Adrienne
April 11, 2019

Forever is composed of nows.
Emily Dickinson

PROLOGUE
Origins of Intentional Living

Let's Start at the Beginning

My intention is for this book to be a beautiful guide for you to connect with yourself in a deeper and more intentional way so you may show up in this world from an inspired and empowered place. As we embark on this adventure together, it feels important to share with you why I may be a worthy companion to you on this journey. I don't pretend to know everything. In fact, I'm wildly imperfect and take great delight in my rawness. What I do know, is that living intentionally, in alignment with my deepest joy, saves my life every day. It is a nourishing and fulfilling life force and it's a pleasure to share it with you.

When I show up as my most authentic self, it gives you permission to do the same. We all have raw material in our lives and it's what we choose to do with it that matters most.

I'm not the first person to discover intention setting. I didn't invent it. But, I did come to learn this and to practice it on a very deep level. I didn't know that it had a name or might already be a *thing*. Once I knew it deep within myself, I could recognize it in the world around me. Suddenly, support for this way of living entered my sphere. I was fascinated.

I have a voracious appetite for this kind of content. I realized through books, podcasts, conversations, social media and a variety of other sources that intentional living has deep roots in many of our technologies—spiritual, scientific, physiological, genetic and so on. It is elemental to our human experience and to our consciousness. With that, I want to briefly share some background with you, but the sheer extensiveness of this topic blows my mind (that's another book).

In this introduction, I want to share with you how I came to discover intention setting in my own life. I will also cite a few of my favorite voices on the topic to give you a sense of the many facets of this diamond. There is so much supporting its validity but what I really want is for you to experience it. I want you to know the context (and perhaps share my curiosity) —but more importantly—I want you to be in this moment and every moment of your life. I want you to breathe, connect and listen. I want you to strip away all that doesn't serve you and come back to the simplicity of showing up in this moment in an intentional way.

My intention with this book is to do three things: (1) I want to tell you what intention setting is, how it's transformative and why it's worth it; (2) I'm going to share with you *how* to be intentional. I will give you simple strategies that you can layer into your everyday in meaningful ways; (3) I've created a whole new set of beautiful intentions for you to bring into your heart and your day. You can choose one at random or on purpose and have it be the theme for your day. It is a pleasure to have you on this intentional journey with me and I hope that you love the ride.

The Origins of My Own Intentional Living

I want to share with you how I came to be so deeply invested in joy and the practice of intention setting. It's not something I chose to study, nor did I ever dream I would share this with the world. It came to me during the worst period of my life. I would come to learn it by standing on the threshold of the rest of my life knowing that there had to be a different way. A much better way.

There was a myriad of possible contributors to my downfall— among them stress, genetics, a sense of inadequacy, high demands, an immobilizing inability to deal with my thoughts and feelings, poor coping strategies and an insatiable desire for love, acceptance and acknowledgment. The result was a complete disconnection of my mind, body and spirit. I struggled with anxiety and debilitating panic attacks. I had complete dis-ease in the world, and I remedied all of it (the good, the bad, the ugly) with a lot of alcohol.

I remember standing in my bedroom one morning eight or nine years ago getting ready for another day in the corporate world. I was zipping up my polka dot pencil skirt. Morning chaos buzzed around me and I was already exhausted by the day's to-dos. For whatever reason, something stopped me in my tracks. I looked out my window and up to the sky and asked, "Is this *it*?" This question surprised me because it felt like abruptly pulling off the highway of my life and putting my car in park. This big question came from a deep and unfamiliar place inside me. *Was this really "it"? Was this living? Is this why I was on this planet and is this what I would do over and over for the next 20 years or so?* It couldn't possibly be.

I snapped myself out of it and returned to my life on overdrive managed by a steady stream of alcohol and Lorazepam. I would drink to be socially comfortable and to extinguish my pain, anger and frustration. I would intentionally drown out all parts of me because they seemed too unmanageable and uncontainable. I thought this substance would bring me the peace and calm I craved so desperately.

Many people ask me when things got so bad, and I really don't know. I slid for a long time. Then, I slid far and fast. Until one day, I found myself crumpled on my bedroom floor shaking, crying and unable to move. How had it come to this? I didn't understand how everyone else was "normal" and I couldn't hack life. I was riddled with shame. I felt desperate and alone. Everything hung in the balance—my marriage, my job, my very existence.

At that time, I would regularly hear a very quiet, consistent voice. It did not rage at me like addiction did. It said, "Adrienne, you need to come home," and "You need to do this by yourself. For yourself." It didn't make sense and yet, there was deep truth and comfort there. It felt like a source of silent strength and I chose to pay attention.

My world felt small and tenuous. I knew I needed help. I think the hardest part was the shame of admitting my life was in complete shambles. Once I'd outted myself, I was under a microscope, exposed and accountable. Worst of all, I was completely raw and vulnerable with no immediate coping mechanisms.

In AA's *Big Book*, the disease of alcoholism is described as "cunning, baffling and powerful," and I couldn't agree more. It wants to keep you in solitary confinement and it's wildly powerful. Breaking out of the cell feels impossible and ludicrous.

The most frightening thing I ever did was admit I had a serious drinking problem and it was out of my control. I exited my life stage left and went to a 21-day treatment program. I remember laying on my back on what felt like a 2-inch thick mattress on a piece of plywood and thinking to myself, the next time I spend thousands of dollars to go somewhere, I don't want it to be here.

I met women of all ages in that facility. One woman's face was collapsing because of prolonged drug use. Another woman was in the throes of getting married to make $35k for drug money. An older woman would only wear shirts buttoned right up to her neck because she was so tormented by the sexual abuse she'd endured as a young girl. Do you know what I saw? I saw incredible, raw beauty. This is where I dropped my shoulders for the first time and was completely honest. It felt like freedom. I had sat at many impressive tables over the years—those of global corporate boardrooms and some of the world's finest restaurants. Yet, this one really struck me because it was the most honest, genuine, authentic and human sharing I had ever experienced.

If you think going to rehab sucks, try re-entering the real world completely sober. While I was grateful on one hand that I could slink back in quietly because I was fragile, on the other hand, I thought *I've just gone through this major life event and we're not going to talk about it?*

While I am grateful for the many resources that were available to me, I found that many of them wanted to bring me back to ground zero, stabilize me and keep me there. There were lots of rules and fear-based statistics bandied around. There was one that stated something like 2% of people who don't go to AA are able to sustain recovery.

In those early days, I was supposed to find a sponsor. I remember having a phone call with a woman who seemed like a good fit for me. I hadn't been to many meetings that week because my husband was out of town. I was finding peace in the small moments. I was cherishing time with my kids and I'd even done a big presentation at work without a panic attack (a remarkable feat for me). I was working with what I had, and I felt deeply content—even "happy"—for the first time in a long time. This sponsor promptly interrupted me, saying I wasn't serious about my recovery because I hadn't been to the requisite number of meetings. Then came the kicker: she didn't really believe it when people said they were "happy."

I hung up on her, pounded my fists against my steering wheel, and I cried harder than I've ever cried (and I've cried a lot). I was so sick of the bullshit. Mine and everyone else's. If I was going to go to all this trouble then I wanted to be happy. In fact, I wanted to be deeply joyful *forever*. I refused to be defined by my worst moments. If that meant being part of the 2%, then I thought *Let's roll up our sleeves and get to work raising that statistic* (where do they interview people for these surveys anyways?).

In that moment, I chose me, and I chose to love myself and my life. I chose joy and I have never looked back.

I didn't need more rules. I needed to excavate my trauma and take care of myself. I read voraciously. I found an excellent therapist and a naturopath. My doctor was very supportive. I worked with energy healers and a shaman. I amped up my yoga practice and cultivated mindfulness and gratitude practices. The people in my life showed me their true colors. Some by loving me and some by leaving me, and I am grateful for all of it. I carved out serious time for my own self-care. I constantly reminded myself that I was right where I was supposed to be and that I was enough. I was grateful to be alive and I knew I was OK.

Joy is a choice. We can choose it in a million different ways every day. How will I talk to myself? What will I eat? What will I choose to have in my social media feed? Who will I spend my time with? What adventures will I have? I choose. You choose.

Happiness is more fleeting while joy is a strong undercurrent of fulfillment that we cultivate and align with. I say this because it's important to note that choosing joy doesn't mean we're happy all the time. Life still happens but now I show up for it in a very different way.

To celebrate five years of sobriety and the completion of my separation, I went to Bali. I was scared to go and ridiculously grateful that I had the freedom to have this adventure. As I lay on my yoga mat surrounded by humid lushness, I cried tears of immense gratitude. I thought about lying on that bed in rehab and marveled at how the Universe works. In that moment, I collected all the pieces of myself, hugging it all in and felt very whole.

I am very grateful for *all* of it. I would not be sharing this with you if it weren't for all of it.

Today, I'm proud to be Chief Joy Curator at this beautiful company I've created, May You Know Joy. I have studied at a Master Coach level with Martha Beck and had the good fortune to receive some of the greatest, toughest life and writing challenges from this renowned writer and mentor. I have intensely studied yoga at a teacher level, and not only can my body do incredible things, but we are friends now. I also thought that my addiction was my mountain to climb but that only gave me the strength and fortitude I needed to navigate a divorce, leave the corporate world and take everything I'd learned forward.

Today, I am a happy, independent, single mom who shows up (perhaps too) authentically for her kids. I am grateful for my incredible network of friends and the many amazing places my work takes me. I am grateful that my card products have resonated with people worldwide and that my e-mail is full of stories of how these cards are changing people's lives. I share this work with people through workshops, retreats, online communities and public speaking. When I'm not pinching myself, I'm just breathing, taking it all in and feeling deeply grateful.

I have learned that when I share this story, it gives you permission to share and we heal together. We are all on this journey together. We are all recovering and reclaiming our truest, most authentic selves. We are questioning and breaking the molds that society wants to put us in. We need to love ourselves—*hard*. And trust ourselves. We need to do the next right thing and have deep faith.

Living joyfully means showing up from a place of integrity. It means being intentional and living on purpose. It also means feeling all of it. While pain can be great, joy is really something else. While living this way asks a lot of a person, the rewards are beyond compare. Magical even. It's freedom. Life is meant to be *lived*.

Living intentionally means showing up mindfully and consciously in each moment. We decide we are going to show up from a place of deep love, gratitude and kindness. No matter what the world throws at us, we choose this experience and this way of being for ourselves. It's all these small moments of choosing that have the most profound effect.

Life is full of rich experiences. Our big, bold, beautiful moments. Our quiet, intimate moments. Our heart wrenching failures, tragedies, traumas and troubling times, timeless experiences and lessons, and yet we need to discover them for ourselves. I didn't know this was called intention setting. I just started showing up for myself every day in gentle and kind ways. Over time this practice has evolved into words, sentences, cards, talks, workshops and this book. This is my life's work and I am grateful to share it with you. No matter where you are on your life's journey, you have this moment to connect to your deepest sense of self and show up in this world with a reverence for your life and all of life. Show us what love and light look like emanating from you.

I am a sample size of one. From the books, teachers, podcasts and tens of thousands of people I've talked to, I know I am not the only one. I wish to contribute to this conversation. This is my thread in the tapestry of our universal experience. I invite you to take what resonates and make it your own.

As I share this with you, I have had 2,615 intentional days (since the day I stopped drinking). In these pages, I offer you my interpretation of what it means to live intentionally. I share it with you because it is transforms me every single day. If you are seeking greater connection with yourself and the world around you, I invite you to listen to your deepest truths and show up in this world intentionally—from a place of love, kindness and gratitude. It is a simple practice that we do without expectation. We do it because it fills us up. It creates our experience. I can tell you, unequivocally, that there are incredible rewards and your life will open in ways you never could have imagined.

Reading these words plants the seeds in your heart and mind. However, the seeds only grow through your tending to them. You will only gain knowing of this practice through your own intention setting, self-awareness, curiosity, commitment to showing up and consistent re-alignment. Make this practice your own. It is not another to-do list item. It is a gift to yourself in this moment and also to your future self. Live your life. Enjoy yourself. Show up as the fullest expression of all you have to offer. It will be courageous, beautiful, inspiring and likely messy. You need you like this and so does the rest of the planet. Let's be wildly imperfect and show up intentionally because of and in spite of it all.

With this book, I offer you what I have learned so far. I hope that I have many years to continue this practice and share it with you. It has been my greatest lesson and I aspire to breathe life into it every day. May you do the same. I wish you joy in your life, grace in each step, a lifetime of intentional days and the rich experience of showing up and creating a life on purpose.

Origins in Spirituality

People have been living intentionally for thousands of years. We can look to the world's great spiritual healers, yogis, Buddhist monks, Qigong masters and shaman for evidence of these transformational processes and their profound effects.

The classic Vedic text known as the *Upanishads* declares,

> *"You are what your deepest desire is. As your desire is, so is your intention. As your intention is, so is your will. As your will is, so is your deed. As your deed is, so is your destiny."*

Deepak Chopra, who explores the power of intention toward manifesting your dreams in his book *The Seven Spiritual Laws of Success*, has this to say:

> *"An intention is a directed impulse of consciousness that contains the seed form of that which you aim to create. Like real seeds, intentions can't grow if you hold on to*

them. Only when you release your intentions into the fertile depths of your consciousness can they grow and flourish."

Marianne Williamson, a renowned spiritual leader, author and activist whose work is rooted in *A Course in Miracles* says:

"Every thought creates form on some level and ... our physical experience is a reflection of our thoughts.

"Nothing binds you except your thoughts; nothing limits you except your fear; and nothing controls you except your beliefs."

My favorite yogi for our times, Guru Singh (who studied under Yogi Bhajan), has this to say:

"When you use your pure intentions over your senses—it does not pave the road to hell, but creates roads beyond your limits—ones that are unlimited. You begin operating on this Earth for heaven's sake, where your life skills fulfill their purpose; where your purpose is driven by passions; where your passion serves all living creatures and finds its greatest reward in doing so."

For yogis and other spiritual lineages, teachings were passed down orally through generations and learned through lesson upon lesson over lifetimes. Failure was revered as the ultimate signal of growth, and enlightenment was a lifelong devotion. The journey was revered, committed to and honored. Today, so many of us hold back because we're afraid to fail. I have found my downfalls to be my greatest teachers. In a yoga class, I once heard a teacher say that the only failure is not taking the lesson. That landed deep in my heart and I often return to that.

The average person can't leave their day job to seek enlightenment. That is why I propose re-packaging the wisdom of intentional living in a beautiful and simple way that meets the needs of our times. The spiritual leaders who have come before us serve as wise guides and examples of the importance of these pursuits. They show us what's possible and offer us great wisdom. Times may change and life my be hectic, yet some truths remain eternal. They are meant to be experienced, learned and re-awakened as part of our evolving human experience.

More recently, Dr. Wayne Dyer spoke and wrote extensively on the subject in *The Power of Intention*. Dr. Dyer begins his exploration of the topic with this beautiful passage:

> *"If you've ever felt inspired by a purpose or calling, you know the feeling of Spirit working through you. Inspired is our word for in-spirited. I've thought long and hard about the idea of being able to access seemingly dormant forces to assist me at key times in my life to achieve an inner burning desire. What are these forces? Where are they located? Who gets to use them? Who is denied access? And why?"*

Thich Nhat Hanh, Zen master, global spiritual leader, poet and peace activist offers us this wisdom on the powerful effect of our thoughts:

> *"When you produce a thought that is full of understanding, forgiveness, and compassion, that thought will immediately have a healing effect on both your physical and mental health and on those around you. If you think a thought that is full of judgement and anger, that thought will immediately poison your body and mind and the people around you."*

While this is only a sampling of this topic, the sentiments shared demonstrate the profound importance and timeless power of our thoughts and intentions. Throughout history, the greatest spiritual leaders have recognized and lived by the power of focussing their attention on living intentionally.

Yet, most of the people I meet tell me "intention setting" is new to them. They've never given it much thought, taken the time to understand it nor applied it to their own lives. This is a powerful, life-sustaining exercise that needs to be practiced. It is not another to-do list item but a meaningful and effective way of being in the world.

Origins in Science

If the life and kinetic abilities of shaman and yogis don't satisfy your innately skeptical and rational mind, science capably steps up with evidence supporting the power of our thoughts. While I was struggling with addiction, my monkey mind was powerful, erratic and destructive. In becoming more intentional in my thoughts, daily practices and self-care, I have restructured my thinking. I now feel the clarity and peace I was seeking. By navigating from this centered place, my perspective has shifted and my experience of the world has opened in amazing ways.

A few of the fields of study that have done extensive research in this area include (but aren't limited to) neuroscience, quantum physics, psychology and epigenetics. Probably the most notable and relevant work related specifically to intention setting is Lynne McTaggart's book *The Intention Experiment* published in 2007. Not only is this book steeped in scientific evidence and the exploration of consciousness, but McTaggart leverages her vast network of readers worldwide to continually perform experiments exploring the power of group consciousness.

As McTaggart explains in the introduction of *The Intention Experiment* and repeatedly proves in this compelling book:

> *"The Intention Experiment rests on an outlandish premise: thought affects physical reality. A sizable body of research exploring the nature of consciousness, carried on for more than thirty years in prestigious scientific institutions around the world, show that thoughts are capable of affecting everything from the simplest machines to the most complex living beings. This evidence suggests that human thought and intention are an actual physical 'something' with the*

astonishing power to change our world. Every thought we have is a tangible energy with the power to transform. A thought is not only a thing; a thought is a thing that influences other things."

She shows the power of intention setting can be traced to early studies in quantum physics:

"The implications of these early experimental findings were profound: living consciousness somehow was the influence that turned the possibility of something into something real. The moment we looked at an electron or took a measurement, it appeared that we helped to determine its final state. This suggested that the most essential ingredient in creating our universe is the consciousness that observes it. Several of the central figures in quantum physics argued that the universe was democratic and participatory—a joint effort between observer and observed."

Through countless examples from group prayer to controlled laboratory experiments to case studies from the world of sports, McTaggart offers rich research on the power of our thoughts and their electromagnetic fields to the direct results they have on other particles, beings, experiences and even performance.

Psychology is also in on the game. Dr. Seligman's work in Positive Psychology is a primary example. In short, his work demonstrates the power that optimism and pessimism can have in affecting our minds and our lives. His evidence suggests that what we pay attention to and how we pay attention are powerful. We can use our thoughts to ends that are either creative or destructive.

We've just grazed the tips of icebergs of research. The breadth and depth of scientific research that proves the power of human thoughts in affecting our experience and our world is extensive, vast and difficult to argue with. If the science behind intention setting piques your curiosity (as it does mine), I encourage you to explore these fascinating works further.

Origins in Mindfulness

Mindfulness has gained wide acceptance in recent decades and this provides a powerful platform for the introduction of intention setting. It is our ability to be mindful in the present moment that allows us to make conscious, intentional choices for ourselves.

The trailblazer and prominent voice in this field is Dr. Jon Kabat Zin. In 1990, he introduced the world to mindfulness and its profoundly positive effects on our daily experience in his book *Full Catastrophe Living*. Since then, the world has embraced mindfulness, and now mindfulness-based stress reduction (MBSR) programs are used in medical centers worldwide.

Jon Kabat Zin explains mindfulness this way:

> *"The practice of mindfulness involves finding, recognizing, and making use of that in us which is already OK, already beautiful, already whole by virtue of our being human—and drawing upon it to live our lives as if it really mattered how we stand in relationship to what arises, whatever it is.*
>
> *"Mindfulness is essentially about relationality—how we are in relationship to everything, including our own minds and bodies, our thoughts and emotions, our past and what transpired to bring us, still breathing, into this moment—and how we can learn to live our way into every aspect of life with integrity, with kindness toward ourselves and with wisdom."*

The research surrounding mindfulness and its effects are impressive and extensive. Mindfulness and meditation have even been used in maximum security prison settings worldwide and in some of the roughest schools to transform and calm the toughest minds.

Intention setting uses mindfulness as a springboard. With mindful awareness, we are empowered to make intentional choices, shifting our experience in ways that are meaningful and purposeful. Intention setting is mindfulness in action.

A Final Word

Summing up these origins and influences in only a few brief pages is my effort to capture and share the vastness of this topic. I will study it for my entire lifetime and likely just scratch the surface. But again, my interest is in sharing the nuances of my personal lived experience of being intentional so that you may know and enjoy its many benefits in your day-to-day life.

SECTION ONE

INTENTIONAL LIVING

When you realize that every stressful moment you experience is a gift that points you to your own freedom, life becomes very kind.

                                                Byron Katie

The arduous yet essential task leading to a tangent of a tangent is the morphing of intention to match the outcomes and then allowing outcomes to be steps to greater outcomes. This is the adventure of allowing image to transform at the heart level—the basic key to changing character through the characteristics.

                                                Guru Singh

What are Intentions?

Life is meant to be lived. Can we breathe into this very moment? Can we connect to our deepest truth, our integrity, our core values and our highest sense of self? Can we honor our feelings and our experiences? Can we meet this moment with our full selves in a mindful, conscious and purposeful way? Can we know deeply that we are connected to the creative forces within us and all around us? Can we harness these forces to be intentional in our moments, ourselves, our relationships and in our world?

Intention is a conscious choice from within and the mindful exercising of that choice. Intention is personal activism in alignment with our deepest, most peaceful truth and our highest purpose for our greatest good. It is the conscious creation of a soulful life.

Intentional living is also the antidote to life on autopilot. It's about being in the present moment and creating our lives on purpose. It is about being curious, raw and honest with ourselves. It's about being authentic and wildly alive. It is about rising up and embracing life as an incredible adventure and each moment as a rich opportunity. Let's get off our hamster wheels. Let's question our patterns. Let's be creative participants in life instead of just going through the motions.

Intention setting is all about choosing. We choose how we want to *be* in this world. Choosing is an act of taking our power into our own hands and deciding how we want to show up, what words we use and how we carry ourselves. If there were only three intentions we could ever choose to motivate all our actions, they would be love, kindness and gratitude. Imagine a world where every person showed up from this place.

Living in our truth means we get clear on who we are and who we want to be. Admittedly, this can be easier said than done. It is an ongoing practice that strengthens over time. Getting back to our true selves means we get re-centered on our core values. A daily intentional practice will help with this, and the "how-to" is in the next section of this book, so you're going to learn how to do this. It's integral to our well-being. From a young age, we get inundated with messages about what we should do and how we should behave to be acceptable and lovable. We need to take a keen look at the "shoulds" in our lives and decide what we are going to do. Instead of reacting to the world and trying to meet its insatiable demands, I'm inviting you to get centered and respond to the world from this calm and mindful place.

In our chaotic world fraught with fear and superficial pressures, intention setting invites us to get back to our essence. When we are true to ourselves and operate from this centered place, conversations shift, energy shifts and we can consciously create our experience. Intention setting can constitute very small acts that may seem inconsequential in the moment, but their cumulative effects—over a lifetime or through a population—can be profoundly transformative. When we take matters into our own hands and hearts with intention and purpose, a world of possibilities opens.

We are Already Whole

Before we dive further into intentions, I want to remind you that we are already whole. This moment is perfect and as Rumi said, "Life is rigged in your favor." Embrace yourself and this moment. You are in charge and it's a gift to wield this much power.

A client once described her thoughts as her internal board of directors. I love this metaphor. She also shared that based on their previous conversations, she didn't like the attitudes, tones or messages coming from this advisory team. We laughed. Since she was in charge, she had chosen to fire them! She was going to assemble a board that she admired and that would support her in creating her most meaningful life.

I loved her conviction about this profound internal change she'd decided to make. This is true for all of us. We are in charge. Let's remember that and come back to it. Let's accept ourselves with kindness and compassion knowing that we're right where we're supposed to be and that each moment can be looked at as a challenge or an opportunity. Let's assemble all our internal and external resources that support us in our deepest intentions and our biggest dreams.

Do you need to make some staffing changes to your own board of directors? I've had to clean house many times!

Living Inside Out

It's easy to find ourselves exhausted and depleted as we desperately attempt to seek love, approval and acceptance outside of ourselves. External expectations are insatiable and can have us easily feeling like we're not good enough. Our 24/7 culture perpetuates this fractured and depleting way to live.

If we really want to live our best lives, we must set the terms and conditions. We must quiet the noise and go inside ourselves. We must get clear on our values and what feels purposeful to us. We don't need to know our life's purpose (that can be a tall order), but we can be purposeful in the actions of our daily lives.

Imagine getting centered at the core of your being and having every action, movement, word and feeling emanate from that place. This is to live intentionally—to radiate from your power center. When we shift our inner lives, the effects on our outer lives are exponential. Our outer world is a direct reflection of our inner world.

Let's consider the alternative for a moment. If we are at our center and let external forces push us and manipulate us, we have the life force energy squeezed out of us. We shrink. We contract. Instead of oppressive energy pushing toward the center, we want to create powerful energy that radiates out from our center. Instead of reacting to the world, we want to respond to it from a place of consideration, integrity and purpose.

The Gifts of Our Deepest Knowing

The greatest gift we can give ourselves is connecting, trusting and living into our deepest sense of knowing. In a world that is ripe with distractions, this sensibility is easy to ignore. We become defined by our busy-ness and numbing is both glorified and readily available. While connecting to ourselves may initially feel daunting and uncomfortable, we can go here by befriending ourselves. There is an essence deep inside that already knows its purpose. It knows how to function. It is already joyful and at ease. Our thoughts, "shoulds," pressures and societal expectations have led us away from this place. We have mistakenly put our faith in things outside of ourselves. I'm suggesting that we find gentle, enjoyable ways to return to who we really are and show up from that place in a million small ways every day.

All Our Moments

I once heard that we have 70,000,000,000 cells and that our heart beats approximately 100,000 times a day. What if we thought of how miraculous all of this is and how it all adds up to one incredible body and one amazing day on Earth? While these cells and heartbeats in isolation are extremely small, think of them collaborating, reproducing and sustaining our very existence. These heartbeats occur on their own and give us life.

So it is with intentions. Each intentional act can feel small. We may wonder if it's worth it or why we should even bother. Our ego wants some reaction, feedback or positive result. What if we trusted that millions of intentional acts would create an incredible, sustainable and fulfilling life? And—think of the heart beats—each one is an opportunity. What if you thought of today as 100,000 opportunities to be truly present in this world? The heart is also the most awesome metaphor for love and life. Not only does it give us life with every heartbeat (something that's not on your to-do list, I might add), it is also the ultimate act of giving and receiving.

The Seeds of Our Intentions

There is an old parable of the world (or the Kingdom of Heaven) being in a mustard seed. It is said that the mustard seed is the smallest of the seeds, and yet when planted in a field grows to be a big tree. Great and vast things can grow from the tiniest of beginnings. These are like our intentions. Each intentional thought, word and action, while seemingly small, can have cumulative, rippling and powerful effects beyond what we can imagine.

We choose the seeds of our intentions and hold them in our hands, honoring them. We release and plant these seeds (our intentions) because they are aligned with our highest good. We want to live a true and authentic life from a place of rich integrity. These tiny seeds already have trees inside of them. They are destined for growth and greatness.

Some seeds will be carried by the wind, but like fertile soil, sunshine and water nourish plants, we need to tend to our intentions—nurturing them and helping them to grow.

There are seeds inside seeds, worlds inside worlds and growth upon growth. The potential is infinite. We need to honor the tininess of the seed and nourish it into fullness.

We need to remind ourselves that everything in nature is intentional. Everything has a much greater, divine purpose. Every seed has the potential to become a beautiful flower or an abundant fruit tree. Nature takes its time and grows and moves through seasons and cycles. We could benefit from getting back to that place, connected to our roots, our truest sense of self and our highest, intentional potential. Can we navigate the seasons with patience?

The seeds of your intentions hold immense hope. The power of these possibilities and your ability to create them in your own life cannot be underestimated. Trust that you are supported. Allow the seeds to grow into something even greater than your wildest imagination can come up with. It is available to you if you are open and allow for it.

Anatomy of an Intention

Another way to imagine this is to liken it to our solar system. The core of your intention is the sun, and planets (the aspects of intentional living) are in orbit around it. (This was the inspiration for the cover illustration and yet, like all of life, this illustration also evolved into something far more interesting, intricate and beautiful.)

The Sun or Core of Our Being – Truth

The core of our being is our deepest sense of truth and knowing. This is our essence. It is who we really are before the world layered on "shoulds," rules about what is acceptable and what we need to do to be lovable. In stillness, we return to this place. Our intuition is here and so are our gut instincts. From this deep center, we are connected to everything. From this true, pure place, we are connected to our personal power and the best of us can radiate out to the world.

Layer 1 – Awareness

Our greatest tool is our awareness. When we are fully conscious, we awaken to our truth, our deepest being and to all our senses. Complete awareness allows us to be present with the fullness of the moment. We begin dropping our filters, fixed ideas and limiting beliefs. We gain clarity and we can show up in the world with curiosity and wonder. From this place, we have more information available to us and we can respond to the world around us from a more peaceful and empowered center. When we are aware, we know the truth. We are open to everything around us and we honor our feelings, our sensations, our deep knowing and our environment.

Try this to connect to awareness: Pause at least one time per day (ideally three or more times) and breathe deep into your belly. Unfurrow your brow and drop your shoulders. Take in where you are, what you are doing and how you are feeling. Notice what comes up and try not to judge it. Just notice and take it in for a minute or two.

Layer 2 – Love

The greatest gift in this lifetime is love. When truth and awareness are nourished with love, they are honored. From this intensely supported place they can be activated in alignment with our highest experience. We begin by loving ourselves. I know this can be tough. But, try it— even a little bit at a time. Flex this muscle. Loving ourselves is an act of grace. When we love ourselves—all of us, exactly as we are—we open up to a world of possibilities. Like a beating heart, we are in alignment with the flow of love—engaging in the world through the expansive cycle of giving and receiving.

Try this to connect to love: Place one hand on your heart and one hand on your belly. Close your eyes and send love and compassion to yourself.

Layer 3 – Kindness

Kindness is a manifestation of love. Our intentions are genuine acts of kindness. They are a generous contribution to our world. They are a demonstration that we are in service to ourselves, our fellow people, the environment, our planet and this experience. Kindness is not manipulative or compromising. We start with ourselves. Can we be kinder to ourselves? Can we treat ourselves and speak to ourselves in a loving and compassionate way? Can we treat ourselves like we would treat our best friend? Once we're kind to ourselves, can we bring this into our interactions with the world?

Try this to connect to kindness: In any given moment, ask "What is the kindest thing I could do for myself in this moment?"

Layer 4 – Gratitude

Gratitude is an amplifying force. It is an act of reverence for everything we are, everything we have and all our experiences. Gratitude grounds us in the now and is a great act of honor. We are open to what is available to us, we witness it, we recognize it and we express deep thanks. A simple daily gratitude practice can be very powerful.

Try this to connect to gratitude: At the end of each day, reflect on three things you are grateful for from the day.

Layer 5 – Wholeness & Acceptance

There is a wealth of personal power in accepting and honoring our wholeness. We carry lightness and darkness. We have joy, pain, bliss, sadness, anger, complacency, grief, peace and contentment. They are all here in the sandbox playing and vying for our attention. Our wellbeing and most intentional life depend on us recognizing that we are all of it. We can have all of these perceived successes and failures. What is important is that we recognize the parts for what they are. They are all signals and guideposts. This raw material is ours to work with, nourish and mold. It's what we create from it that's important.

Try this for connecting to acceptance: In any situation, ask "How could this be happening *for* me?"

Layer 6 – Choice

When we are in our truth, fully aware and standing in our wholeness, we have the power to choose. We can take the raw material of our lives—a situation or this very moment—and choose what to do with it. We are creators. We will choose what kind of person we want to be, how we want to show up in the world and what kind of experience we want to create while we're on this planet. We will be tested of course. We will choose again, course correct, re-align and strengthen our commitment in doing so.

Try this for connecting to choice: Is this choice in alignment with my core values?

Layer 7 – Commitment

It is fascinating to stop and take stock occasionally. When we connect back to our truth and our core values, we align with what we really want to create for ourselves. What do we want to commit our days, our time and our lives to? What kind of legacy do we want to actively live while we are on this planet? What do we want to dedicate ourselves to? What do we want to take responsibility for creating?

When we get grounded in the commitment to our vision, resolve and endurance will rise to meet it. When we encounter obstacles, pain and frustration, what is it that we are so committed to that we just keep on going? This, my friends, is very powerful.

Try this for connecting to commitment: Write down what you are or want to be committed to. This could be life purpose, relationships, goals and aspirations or any personal cause you are deeply connected to.

Layer 8 – Energy

Our energy is our best resource. There's a saying that where attention goes, energy flows. The question is: Where are we going to focus our energy and our attention? Again, it's a matter of choice and commitment. We decide what we are going to activate and radiate. The other important aspect of energy is nourishing and managing it. It's a resource that we need to mindfully renew so that we are sustainable over the long haul.

There are two important aspects. The first is supporting your energy through diet, exercise, rest, inspiring yourself, having a supportive network and keeping your thoughts clear. The second aspect is using this energy wisely in ways that are intentional and aligned with your purpose.

Try this to connect with energy: How will I nourish my energy today? What am I going to put my energy into?

Layer 9 – Joy

It's important to pause here and remind ourselves that our natural state is uninhibited and wildly expansive joy. While we might be keen to explore and practice the "steps" of being intentional, remember that this is not meant to be a daunting "to-do" list. It's also not a measuring stick of your success (or failure) as a person. There's enough judgement in this world and we're trying to escape it, not feed it.

Being intentional should spring from your well of joy. Delight in being intentional because it feeds your soul. It is fun to show up as we are. We are full of love and gratitude and we are putting our energy into taking care of ourselves and showing up in alignment with our best selves. This is joy. We need it. The world needs it. Can we be intentional from this inspired and empowered place? Can we enjoy the ride and celebrate our time on this planet in big and small ways every day?

Try this to connect with joy: What small things can I integrate into today that connect me with my joy?

Layer 10 – Freedom

All the layers lead us to greater freedom. There is freedom in showing up in this world in a way that is raw, authentic and honest. We have nothing to hide. Shame doesn't live here. When we feel comfortable standing in our own shoes, it is very liberating. To be in service to the world from this place of love, kindness, gratitude and joy is the greatest gift. We benefit and the entire world benefits. Let's not put ourselves into boxes that don't exist. Sometimes we create artificial boundaries. Let's question our limitations and break down walls that we've constructed. Freedom is available to you. Allow yourself to feel it, savor it and revel in it.

Try this to connect to freedom: What thought, action or other inspiration would connect me to my freedom today?

Layer 11 – Openness

At the outermost layer of our intentional being and life is openness. When we show up in the world from this inspired and empowered place, we can be grounded and yet have an open mind and heart. When we're open, we can receive this moment in its fullness. Openness allows us access to more information and greater experiences. Without attachment to a specific outcome, we release our judgement and measurement systems. Suddenly, all things become possible. When I open to infinite possibilities, life becomes way more interesting than anything I could have dreamed up myself.

Try this to connect to openness: When you are talking to people today, can you be open to them in this moment? Can you drop your filters and judgements and really notice who they are right now?

The Power of Presence

The power of the present moment is always available to us. It's really all we have, and it's meant to be savored and really lived. Can we be fully present in this moment?

A yoga teacher once said to me, "Adrienne, inhale to your full expansiveness, exhale completely and go deeper. And—relax." This struck a very deep chord within me. In each moment, could I just expand to what is here? Could I sink into it and give myself permission to go deeper? Could I drop into this moment and what is right here? Could I just relax into it? Could I open myself and find greater ease here?

Everything in the past has already happened. Can we loosen our attachment to it? Can we take this raw material and decide what kind of future we want to create for ourselves? The only failure is not taking the lesson forward.

As for the future, is it possible not to stress ourselves with a million stories about what *could* happen? Can we re-center in this moment and ask ourselves what is the next best thing I can do to create the future I want to align with? It could be so many things. It could be taking action or taking a nap. Let's listen to the moment, to ourselves, and be present to what is actually going on.

Can we leverage all our senses and turn off our expectations? Can we be with this moment exactly as it is and take in everything it offers? Usually, there is much more available to us in the present moment than we ever could have imagined.

The quote on the wall of my yoga studio says: *If you want to be sad, live in the past. If you want to be anxious, live in the future. If you want to be peaceful, live in the now.*

Always Choosing

I want to remind you that you always have the power to choose. You can choose your thoughts, your actions and your words. You can choose to speak up or be quiet, to stay or to go.

We get pulled so far outside ourselves that life can easily become a soul-crushing game of compare and despair. Worse yet, we can find ourselves on autopilot going through the motions, rushing from one thing to the next while this moment—and life in general—passes us by.

I want to encourage you to pause. Be in your body in this moment and make a choice for yourself. How can I take care of myself right now? How can I be kinder to myself and the world around me? What do I want to create in this moment?

Take your power back. Fuel it with some joy and inspiration. Can you savor the deliciousness of this very moment?

Embrace your power to choose.

When I was making horrible choices and no choices at all, I was fully on autopilot numbing out anything that felt mildly uncomfortable. When I realized all the energy I put into my own self-destruction, I wondered: What if I put all this energy into creating the most wonderful moment, experience, day and life I can imagine? That's a powerful shift. You choose how you carry yourself and how you respond to the world. Anything that costs you your peace is a very high price to pay.

Opportunities & Possibilities

Again, intention setting is an opportunity. It's important to restate because we're hard on ourselves. Intention setting is not another measuring stick. We are not asking, Did I do it right? Was I successful? Am I a total failure *again*?

When we set an intention, it's an opportunity to show up and be fascinated with ourselves and the world around us. Will it inspire what you wear, what food you eat, what music you listen to, how you enter a conversation? Be playful and curious and go exploring. This is what it means to be conscious and in perpetual creative response to what is happening.

Where is the opportunity in this moment? What do I want to create for myself? Can I do or say something differently? Play. Notice. Course-correct. There's no right and wrong. It's all information and you can do with it exactly as you choose. Have a little fun with it.

Intention setting is deciding what kind of life we would like to live and what kind of legacy we want to leave. Living intentionally is acting to consciously create our lives on purpose because it is important to us and feels like the most worthwhile endeavor there could possibly be.

Can we re-capture some of our childlike wonder and be curious? Can we practice our intentions? Can we break patterns? Can we shift our experience? Can we notice the results and keep re-aligning? Can we recognize the infinite number of opportunities and possibilities available in each moment?

Living Without Expectations

Living intentionally means we show up because it's important to us personally and it feels worth it. The world may not respond in kind, but we keep showing up intentionally despite that because that's the way we want to live. I know what you're thinking: I'm going to all this effort without expectation? Yes—and read further. There are a few ideas to bear in mind as you digest this.

Our brains are a catalogue of our memories. We know what we've experienced. What if your expectations are too small? What if the outcomes could be much vaster or greater? Also, the brain's core function is to keep us safe, which it does very well. We need to go beyond our brains' safety mechanisms and explore new waters. We need to wade into uncertainty and float on our backs.

Specific expectations also have the potential to lead to disappointment and self-judgement. This will limit the potential of what may be available to us in any given moment or experience. What if what we expect or "want" is not the greatest possible outcome? Instead of defaulting to judgement of the results being "good" or "bad," can we find the information that's available to us? This reminds me of one of my favorite sayings:

The Universe only ever has three answers:
1. *Yes*
2. *Not yet*
3. *I have something better in store*

Combine this with the fact that intentional living is a powerful choice from within. We choose to show up in this way because it is truthful and in clear alignment with our most authentic selves. It's an act of truth, bravery and authenticity. This, in itself, is self-fulfilling already. It is full of joy and power. We are intentional and open to what comes our way because it is always more interesting and rewarding than anything we could have dreamt. Play in the uncertainty and be open to the wonder.

If you're scratching your head and wondering how to get into alignment and how all of these things factor into real life, don't worry. The next section is going to provide you with suggestions on how to layer this into your everyday.

The Universe Will Test You

When you pronounce an intention, you can bet the Universe will say "game on" and give you many opportunities to practice. Are you up to the challenge? Is this something you really want to be aligned with? We live and grow through showing up, through experience and through practice.

Living intentionally is not a practice of perfection. It's a life path. When we get these tests, our results will vary—we'll be awesome, and we'll fall flat on our faces. We'll have good days and bad days. We'll notice, re-align and keep going.

I was using meditation cards daily to help a coaching client bring this practice into her daily life. One day, she e-mailed me at lunch and told me in no uncertain terms that these cards and this whole intention setting thing did not work. She explained that she had been kind *all* morning and had gotten nothing in return. She threw her hands up in disgust.

I sensed her irritability and frustration and it made me smile because it was a signal of her growing awareness. This person wanted something in return. If we want to create kindness in our lives, we need to *be* kind. We're kind because it feels worth it to us. We understand that we won't always get it back. Sometimes we'll touch someone and never know it. Other times, it will come back to us in spades.

If we want to *be* something, we need to *be* it. We need to practice it. We need to model it. We need to test it out. We need to implement, integrate, get feedback and see what the next right step is.

You'll remember that I believe kindness is a foundational intention. Our days are probably begging for more kindness and we can layer it into every aspect. We can take a kind, quiet moment to connect with ourselves before our feet hit the floor in the morning. We can say a kind word to ourselves when we look in the mirror. We can find big and small ways to be kinder to ourselves all day. How will we nourish ourselves? How can we shift our inner dialogue to be kinder? Sometimes we'll find ourselves in toxic situations and the kindest action we can take is to extract ourselves. Kindness can come in lots of shapes and sizes. Figure out what fits for you.

Remember: your intentions are not a success metric. There's no right or wrong way to respond to any given situation. You will practice being intentional in a way that feels truthful and authentic (and that you have the energy for) in any given moment. You are always going to notice how it went and have it influence your next courageous and intentional steps.

How are Intentions Different than Goals?

This is a common question and it's a good one. There is a place for both goals and intentions.

Let's talk about goals first. It is important for us to have goals that are measurable achievements we're working towards. We put energy and resources into reaching these goals. Imagine a triangle with our goal being the upper point. Think of the space between the base and upper point of the triangle being the resources you put into narrowing in on and reaching this goal. We will set big and small goals on a given day, in a given year, and in our lifetime. It's important to be specific about what we want to accomplish, and work toward hitting these targets.

Intentions are similar in that they are something we believe in and want to put our energy into. Now, imagine the intention as an upside-down triangle. Our intention is the bottom point. This is the core of our intention. We are going to put energy into this intention in the way we treat ourselves, in the way we treat other people, and how we show up in the world. In the same way the sides of the triangle widen, when we act intentionally, all sorts of possibilities open up. Our intentions can also be felt far and wide. Sometimes we don't even know the greatness of the impact we can have or what can manifest because of our intentions.

Goals and intentions align us with something greater. They require our attention, time and effort. They may cross paths. They may even be beautiful companions. They have distinct personalities and I invite you to let both thrive in your life.

The Importance of Showing Up

A big part of life is just showing up for it. Not hiding, not waiting until we're *ready* or the conditions are perfect. Maybe there's the possibility of an impending failure or some disappointment; show up anyway.

Life has this amazing way of surprising and supporting us. Start noticing all the stories you make up in your head. What are the scenarios that you've already played out in your mind? Compare this to what actually happens if you show up from a place of intention and openness. The outcome may surprise you.

Connect with a practice that helps you get centered. Maybe it's breath work, a mantra, wearing a special piece of jewellery, carrying a memento with you or listening to your favorite song. Do something that connects you to yourself and reminds you that you will be OK no matter what the outcome. Show up because you believe in yourself and because every experience and relationship is an opportunity to remind you about who you really are.

I had applied to offer a workshop at a women's conference. I'd felt good about pushing myself out of my comfort zone when I'd applied and not so good when it came time to put myself *out there*. All the workshops were to be held on Saturday afternoon at 2 p.m. Prior to that, many impressive, smart and charismatic international speakers had delivered compelling talks. I felt like a nobody and began to wither at the idea that we were all hosting workshops at the same time. I was immediately brought back to the dusty baseball field of my youth where I'd stood many times kicking the dirt waiting for someone to pick me for their team.

As I stood in my room that morning, I questioned the knot in my stomach and the tightness in my throat. Maybe I was getting really sick and should stay in my room. But then, another voice chimed in to counter the fear of my ego. It said, "Adrienne, cut the BS and get out there. This isn't about you. These women are here for their own healing. If they need to hear what you have to say, they will. Otherwise, they will go where they need to. Nobody is going to die. Nothing terrible is going to happen. If no one comes, join another group and enjoy yourself. Just show up."

So, having thoroughly kicked my own ass, I walked down to the central meeting area at 2 p.m. to host my workshop. As I got down there, there was a small and beautiful group of women. They said they'd been waiting for me and my heart nearly burst out of my chest. We had an amazing session that afternoon.

The story gets better. On Monday morning, before I was to leave the conference, I'd carved out time to enjoy the beautiful grounds by walking the labyrinth and meditating for a while. I was grateful I had shown up and was reflecting on that rich lesson. As I stepped away, I met the woman who ran the wellness center. She is someone I admire deeply, and she asked me if I wanted to submit a proposal to deliver workshops the next year. I was ecstatic. Not only had this been an invaluable growth opportunity, but in her, I'd met an inspired collaborator, a mentor and a friend. None of this would have happened had I not shown up. There are exponential gifts for showing up from an intentional place because it feels worth it. We must be willing to grow, to serve and to fall down.

Being in the Discomfort

There is a misconception that being intentional and aligned with joy means that life is like the first day of spring every day. Unfortunately, it's not! However, bad days aren't as paralyzing as they once were and with solid, consistent practices, we can navigate rough waters more swiftly and with greater ease.

You may not want to hear this, but sometimes coming into alignment means being in the discomfort. Life can be challenging, difficult and very uncomfortable. It's not fun, but you need to feel it and let it move through your system. This can be through screaming in your kitchen, venting to a friend, having a dance party or some other physical movement. I can attest to all these! You could also journal, run, go boxing or do whatever activity helps you unleash what is not meant to be bottled up.

My friend and I call it "flailing." This seems counter intuitive to this seemingly Zen-like intentional state we're talking about. But, it's essential. It's real. It's raw and it's authentic. This is the truth trying to get out. Your feelings are wise guides. Let them come up and out.

Be in the discomfort and do the next best thing you can for yourself to help dislodge it. Believe it or not, this awareness and act of self-care is powerful and empowering. Harness it for your greatest good.

Sometimes the discomfort can feel unbearable. It reminds me of giving birth to my daughter. The physical pain was exponentially greater than anything I'd ever felt. I felt like I was going to die that day and the doctor remarking that my body did not respond well to pain didn't help. It was the grossest understatement of my life. But, this baby was coming one way or another. I didn't care at that point if it required a tow truck.

Caterpillars go through a remarkable natural process, too. It's no wonder the butterfly is a such a common metaphor for transformation. These caterpillars don't morph into butterflies. First, they are completely reduced to goo. Have you ever felt like goo? Then, the butterfly forms and still must force its way out of the chrysalis, which is also an arduous natural feat.

I mention these natural birthing processes because they show there is incredible pain and discomfort in birth and transformation. Feel the pain. Trust the process. Know that this is part of the process. Seek support while you're going through it. Allow it to take its course. Don't stop. Keep pushing! It may be the greatest teacher we have.

Purpose

A lot of people struggle with "finding" their purpose. It can feel elusive or too big. In their quest to find it, they can often feel paralyzed into inaction. They feel that until they find it and align with it, they are adrift at sea and life can feel untethered and lacking meaning.

What is your purpose, my purpose, our purpose? Big questions for sure. If you know it and are aligned with it, I invite you to continue to open to it and explore the vastness of opportunities it presents to you.

For those of us who are unsure or less certain, I offer you this: can you be purposeful? Can you leverage this moment, this experience, or this conversation to show up from a purposeful and intentional place? Can you connect with your integrity and explore what it means to show up from this empowered place?

By continually being intentional and purposeful, we are creating purpose and meaning moment by moment. More importantly, we are having a positive impact on the world and the effects are cumulative. The world needs your light. I invite you to play with it and explore it. Take the baby steps and see where they lead you.

Love vs. Fear

Being intentional is expansive. It is not goal oriented as in there is not one destination, one box to check and then it's mission accomplished. Being intentional is like a sun beaming its rays in every direction, filling everywhere with its warmth.

To celebrate five years of sobriety and the completion of my divorce negotiations, I decided to go on a solo trip to Bali. While I was terrified to travel around the world and be in an unknown country on my own, pushing myself way beyond my comfort zone to mark these significant life events felt like I was honoring the next phase of my life and my personal freedom.

While there, I had booked an appointment to see a powerful healer. I tried to cancel the appointment telling myself it was silly and that I shouldn't go all *Eat Pray Love* on myself. Of course, due to a myriad of misalignments (or alignments), I couldn't cancel and found myself in his presence. I hadn't gone with a specific question, but one came up while I was there. "Why am I still so afraid?" It seemed to pop up from some deep place. I hadn't been thinking about it, but it felt true. I had navigated some difficult situations and I was on the other side. I was grateful to have processed my separation in what felt like a true and authentic way. I was in this lush paradise and still my heart felt constricted with fear. Among the many things he shared with me and what resonates to this day are his words: "Do everything from a place of love."

This feels like the true beating heart of being intentional. We can connect with this feeling of deep love, live from this place, allow it to guide us. Love is deep and expansive. It is uninhibited and unconstricted. It allows us to grow into the fullness of ourselves. It is confident and brave and bold and beautiful. Carrying ourselves in the world from a place of love versus fear is a game changer.

Personal Responsibility = Freedom

Being intentional is taking responsibility for our own core values, for our contribution to the world and for the experiences we create.

There was a point when being responsible felt like a heavy weight tied to my ankle. I was tired of being the responsible one. It felt arduous, boring and unfulfilling. It felt like so many people around me were "getting away with" being irresponsible and I wondered why I couldn't, too.

For me, being irresponsible meant numbing out with alcohol and letting that dictate my experience of the world. It meant putting my worth, dreams and acceptance in the hands of others.

Through my downfalls, I learned that personal responsibility is a gift. When I took my power back, I learned to love myself. I could control what I said, how I chose to show up and what I created for myself. I learned that taking responsibility was full of nobility and grace. I also learned that it offered me the gift of personal freedom.

Being intentional can feel like a weighty responsibility. It can feel like you're on a deserted island. But, I invite you to explore what it really feels like to define your own self-worth, dreams, and terms and conditions in the world. While it may feel like an uphill battle some days, you'll find that the view from the top of the hill is well worth the hike to get there.

Sustainability

Living intentionally is like creating the architecture for a rich and sustainable life. If we are intentional in how we take care of our bodies, minds and spirits, they will be nourished, renewed and fulfilled. If we are intentional in how we show up in the world, we will model for others what this means. We will create meaningful experiences for ourselves and for the lives of those we touch.

In living this way, we also set up support systems. We set up daily practices, coping mechanisms and a network of people who support us. While the baby steps of cobbling this together can seem random or small, the significance is not to be underestimated. By creating these systems, we create a powerful web of support. Then, when life happens (as it is guaranteed to), we can access these resources to facilitate our journey.

Be on Your Own Side

Given that I've got some 2,000+ intentional days under my belt, you might be relieved to know that intentional living comes in particularly helpful on tough days or longer stretches of hardship.

I have found that when tough days strike, my commitment to being intentional becomes even stronger. It becomes essential. I slow down and ask myself "How can I best support myself right now?" and "What is the next best thing I can do?" I am mindful of each step.

On the tough days, I'm particularly mindful of how I take care of myself and usually amp this up. I'm very aware of staying present, keeping my thoughts in check, being intentional in my actions and drawing on the support of my trusted network. I've found it invaluable to have people around me who know me inside out, who I trust, who offer advice when I ask for it and who know how to gently guide me back to myself. It is a deliberate practice — this exercising of intentional self care and seeking out support.

I can't count the number of times these muscles have been broken down and strengthened during challenging times.

While I knew my divorce was for my greatest good, it didn't mean it was without fierce emotions, frustration and wild uncertainty. I once came out of a meeting with my ex and our lawyers and I was so angry that when I got home, I just stood in my kitchen and screamed as loud as I could. With that violent eruption, I knew I needed to get really intentional about the way I was going to handle the next several months. I could *go* through this or I could *grow* through it.

I got intentional with my health and ensured I was mindful about who I confided in and received guidance from. I got amazing counselling on clearing my emotions and handling myself with integrity (particularly during challenging conversations). The other aspect that seemed daunting was all the paperwork (financial, etc.). How was I going to navigate this when I was not a fan of budgeting to begin with? I sat at my computer and thought that I needed to approach this in a way that felt inspiring and like I was on my own side (not just keeping my head above water).

With that, an idea came, and I decided to label my entire divorce file "The Freedom Project." Every new action I took toward the dissolution of this marriage felt intentional and in alignment with my highest good. I told my lawyer that this was the only way we would refer to these "proceedings," and while I'm sure she thought I was crazy, she seemed to be entertained by the idea. She told me that I was her only client who signed documents in gold marker! As I worked on "The Freedom Project" on a regular basis I could complete all the related tasks in small steps with a sense of purpose and lightness in my heart. The kitchen screaming (while elemental to my progress) was no longer necessary.

On your tough days, I encourage you to ramp up the self-love and self-compassion. Be on your own side. Collect people who are also on your side. Not gossipers—only true-blue supporters who have the strength to let you fall apart and encourage you to pick yourself up and keep going.

During these times, taking the next intentional step in alignment with your deepest core values can be the best thing you ever do. These moments add up. You will navigate with greater grace and you will process things as you go. By responding instead of reacting, and by staying very connected to your deepest sense of self, you tether yourself to this moment and a bright future. You don't stay mired in the past.

Being Intentional in a Messed-Up World

You might ask, "How can we be intentional in this messed up world?" I ask, "How can we not be?"

This world can be a fear-based, dangerous and unkind place. Of course, I'm not suggesting you put your personal safety at risk, but what if more of us infused our days and this world with some intentional energy? Imagine the shifts we'd see. It's called paying it forward and it's powerful. We're all in this together.

Being intentional is a powerful energy. When you are grounded and your entire being is in alignment and integrity, that's a powerful place to be. This energy radiates from you and affects those around you whether you personally witness their experience or not. So, your effect on this planet can be profound and widespread in ways that you cannot and probably will not ever begin to imagine. As Ghandi said, *Be the change you wish to see in the world*.

Please don't be paralyzed by fear or worried about doing it wrong. We are creators who are not meant to stand still. We are here to grow, experience life and know deep joy. We need to create hope. Be you. Be here. Be wildly alive. Be part of the solution. Really *be*. And while you're at it, make a difference.

Intentional Days

It can be easy to get caught up in all the busy-ness. Life gets chaotic, and now more than ever, there is so much vying for our attention. It's easy to get disconnected. Before we know it, we are on autopilot spending our days rushing from one thing to the next only to fall into bed exhausted. This is where dis-ease creeps in.

Let's not let that happen. Let's remember Emily Dickinson's words that *Forever is made of nows*. What are we going to do with this moment? What kind of day do we want to create? Let's look at each day with a sparkle in our eye and infuse it with as much goodness as we possibly can. Let's navigate from a place of inspiration and love. Let's be mindful and curious. Let's play.

Just imagine if this caught on. The world would be a more peaceful, healthy and productive place.

Love yourself hard. Show up and live in a wild and passionate way. May each of your days be intentional. You can create your life on purpose.

SECTION TWO

CREATING OUR LIVES ON PURPOSE

And the time came when the risk to remain tight in a bud was more painful than the risk it took to bloom.

Anaïs Nin

Life is rigged in your favor.

Rumi

*The little things? The little moments?
They aren't little to me.*

Jon Kabat-Zinn

Connect. Listen. Integrate.

In speaking to thousands of people, the most common questions I am asked are:
1. What does it really mean to *be* intentional?
2. *How* do I do this?

People tell me that they're too busy and that they don't have time. First, I want to remind you that you are the master of your own time. Time is your creation and you can choose how you will spend it. We all have obligations, but we also have time. Secondly, being intentional is not another to-do list item. You can carve out time, but you don't have to. It is a mindset and a lifestyle choice that can be layered onto every single thing you do. And, perhaps most importantly, wouldn't you agree that spending time to be present, enjoy yourself and create a life on purpose might be deeply satisfying and worth dedicating time to?

I've given a lot of thought to this persistent *how* question. One guidepost insight came to me as I was sitting next to the labyrinth at Grail Springs in Bancroft, Ontario. It was a beautiful summer morning and I was surrounded by trees with prayer flags hanging from the branches. A yellow prayer flag caught my attention and it had the following three words on it: "Connect. Listen. Integrate." Those words softly, yet deeply, landed in my heart and I thought, *Yes, this feels very true. These are the pillars of intention setting.*

We connect to our bodies, minds and spirits. We ensure that our entire instrument is tuned. Once we are aligned in our integrity and intention, we navigate the world with this compass. We connect to family, friends, people, the world and our environment in a meaningful, inspired and intentional way.

Once connected, we listen intentionally. We listen to our bodies, our hearts, our intuition and our truth. We listen to those around us. We listen to our feelings. We listen to the nudges and all wisdom coming to us and allow it to sift until we hear the grains of wisdom that feel deeply true for us. We are fully aware and listening with all of ourselves.

And, we integrate. We integrate our intentions into the fabric of our lives. We integrate intention into how we treat our bodies and what we say to ourselves. We integrate intention into our words and our actions. We integrate it into the essence of our being and show up in the world from this centered, grounded and radiant place. An intention operates at the most cellular and universal levels of our existence.

With this in mind, I offer you two things. First, in this section, I will offer you suggestions as to how to connect with your intentions and how to live intentionally. Second, I offer you complete creative license from that point on. Our brains will always default to the normal patterns they're comfortable with and feel safe in. Exercise your imagination to create new patterns, follow a new path and have big adventures. I don't care what you do, just do something!

What matters most is that you *are* intentional. From this place, I invite you to infuse your intentional living with practices that feel meaningful and joyful to you. Life is meant to be lived, savored and enjoyed. Create practices that you can integrate into your life in big and small ways every day. Create practices that light you up and nourish your soul. Have fun. Create, shift, modify. Invite your friends. Open yourself to the magic and abundance coming your way because if you show up in the world from this place, your joy and fulfilment are inevitable. I promise.

Starting & Ending the Day with Intention

The morning is the most beautiful time to activate your intentions. Everything flows from the source. How you start matters.

When we wake up each morning, we have a blank canvas in front of us and can choose whatever paint colors we wish.

We stretch and wake up to the world, inviting a new day. Today is a day that we're not getting back. What are we going to do with the 24 hours ahead of us? This is a beautiful opportunity to express gratitude for this day, to close our eyes and connect to our deepest sense of self and choose how we want to show up today.

Morning rituals can be seconds, minutes or hours. Any moment can be sacred if we infuse it with love. As a dear friend of mine (and divine creator of the cover illustration) says, intention + love = ritual. I couldn't agree more.

Morning Ritual Ideas

- ❖ Before your feet hit the floor, pause and express gratitude for the new day. Place your hands on your heart and commit to showing up from a place of love and gratitude. Check in with your deepest self and ask what it needs to do to be nourished and to serve today.
- ❖ Morning meditation – Meditation is a centering way to enter the day. At its simplest, you can close your eyes and connect with your breathing. There are also many incredible meditation apps if you wish to be guided, accompanied or otherwise.
- ❖ Morning Movement – Morning movement (yoga, running, walking, stretching or another exercise regimen) can be an intentional way to connect body, mind and spirit, and start the day invigorated and refreshed.
- ❖ Reading – If there is a book, poem or passage that is delicious soul food for you, take time to take this in. This quiet moment is a great act of self-care and is a grounding way to set the tone for your day.
- ❖ Journaling – Writing is an excellent way to process thoughts and emotions. Whether it's a journal with prompts (there are so many good ones), a list of what you are grateful for, or a wish for how you want to show up in the world, write it down. Commit it to paper and to your heart. It doesn't have to sound perfect. It must come from your soul and take the form of written words in the material world.
- ❖ Choose an Intention – Choosing an intention, whether it's with a card, a sentiment from your heart or one of the foundational three (love, kindness or gratitude), sets the tone for your day. It is a way of choosing to be mindful and conscious of how you

want your day to unfold. From this intentional place, you have a compass point with which to align throughout your day.
- ❖ Recite a mantra – Here is one I've created for our mornings:

Morning Mantra

May I be well.
May I be grateful.
May I be kind.
May I find peace and be at ease.
May I ground with deep roots and
Reach out to the vastness of the universe with
Great trust, wild dreams and big love.

Evening Ritual Ideas

- ❖ Reflect – As you unwind from the day, there is an incredible opportunity to create a deeper connection with yourself in a kind and loving way. Take stock of your day. What are you grateful for today? What are you happy to leave behind? What will you do to create a better tomorrow? How did opportunities to practice your intention show up and how did you navigate them?
- ❖ Retire – Create personal time for yourself in the evening. Disconnect from your devices and the world around you. Give yourself a break and allow your mind to shut down.
- ❖ Rest – Create sufficient time for your body to rest and sleep. Our bodies need rest, restoration and rejuvenation. This is the body's work to do at night. While our culture would have you believe otherwise, being "on" 24/7 is not only unsustainable but it's detrimental to our long-term health and mental clarity.
- ❖ Recharge – Take time for self-care. Allow yourself to power down. Listen to the gentle needs of your body, mind and spirit. Be kind to them. Create beautiful rituals out of removing yourself from the world and recharging. Have a bath, read a

good book, listen to a guided meditation. Shift into a much lower gear and allow your body to put its energy elsewhere.
- ❖ Honour the Day – Say a prayer, recite a mantra or cultivate a special ritual of connection to express what's in your heart. Here is one I've created for our nighttimes:

Nighttime Mantra

I am grateful for today.
I honor its abundance and its challenges.
I release what doesn't serve me
and carry the lessons forward.
I breathe deeply, connecting to my deepest sense of self
And my highest love.
I will rest my mind, body and spirit.
I give thanks for all of it.
I invite the darkness
Until morning.

How to Set an Intention

While there are no rules, here are some suggestions to guide you. I invite you to infuse any practice with your essence, your style and whatever brings you a deep sense of joy. Practices can change and evolve over time. The most important part is the practice. Be in your life. Live your life.

Choose Your Intention

- ❖ Connect to your deepest truth and highest desires for your best life. What do you really want to create for yourself? These answers will inspire your intentions.
- ❖ Choose an intention – This can be done any number of ways.
  - You can use a card deck (like the *May You Know Joy* or *Seeds of Intention* decks, and there are so many other good ones)

and choose a card at random (trusting that the Universe has got your back) or on purpose (if there is something specific you are working on or want to manifest).
- Foundational intentions – If there were no other intentions (ever!) I would say we could safely and beautifully operate from the big three: love, kindness and gratitude. Imagine what the world would be like if we all operated from these intentions. If you choose no others, you will be all set with one or all of these.
- Choose your own adventure – You may not need help choosing an intention. You may already know it in your heart. This is also a perfect way to align yourself.

Activate Your Intention

- ❖ Connect with the Intention
  - What is most important is how the intention resonates with you in your heart, body and mind. Connect with why this intention feels true, important and worthwhile.
  - You may want to close your eyes, take a few deep breaths and feel the intention at a deep level.
  - You may want to create a ritual around your intention setting process:
    - Perhaps you have a special, quiet and sacred place to set your daily intentions
    - Perhaps you light a candle
    - Say a mantra, prayer, affirmation or other way of stating your intentions
    - Pause and place your hands on your heart, close your eyes and center the intention into your heart. Breathe deeply into your heart space, fanning the flames of your intention
  - You may want to choose a visual reminder of your intention

- It may be a card from your deck that you carry with you or post in a place that is visible to you throughout the day
- You may wear a special scent that reminds you of the intention
- You may have a piece of jewellery that is your reminder
- You may have a crystal or other natural object that ties you to this intention
- It may be your vision board or a special photograph or piece of artwork
- The visual reminder can take so many shapes and forms—what matters is that it is meaningful to you. It provides you with a beautiful opportunity to shift your focus back to what's important when you feel yourself heading off course

• Write it down – Journaling can be a great way to get out your thoughts, dreams, desires and frustrations. It doesn't have to be long, poetic or ever read again. Be honest and honor your feelings with words written on paper.

• Notice your resistance – It's completely natural to have resistance, so notice it, be aware of it, question it and use it as an opportunity to explore where you can open further into this intention. Answers may not always come immediately. Resistance will create an opportunity for you to grow and growth can take time. Notice, be patient and invite opportunities to explore.

• Physically connect to it – When we are connected to our most intentional self, we are relaxed and joyful. Connect with breathing deep into your belly, relax your face (specifically your brow!), soften your shoulders and unclench your jaw. These are actions that you can return to anytime to create greater awareness and ease in your body. They will also help you release tension and return to a grounded and centered place. Pause periodically throughout your day

(anytime, anywhere) and feel your energy significantly shift by mindfully doing one or all of these actions.
- Be creative – let your imagination and your heart guide you.

Integrate & Practice Your Intentions

You can practice your intention in so many ways. Play, be curious, explore and have fun with it. Remember that this is your own creation for your highest good. Live the intention from this heart-centered place.

- ❖ Self-Love – The creation of an intention is a great act of love in and of itself. To just be here is perfect. This is an act of being grounded in your truth, having reverence for your experience and respecting what you offer the world. To set an intention is to declare at the soul level that you wish to align with the Universe in a meaningful way.
- ❖ Opportunities – The world will present you with a myriad of opportunities to practice being intentional. Show up from this intentional place. Seize the opportunities and use them as an opportunity to show up in a purposeful way.
- ❖ Words – Our words are incredibly powerful. Let's be extra mindful about what we are actually saying. What is the intention behind the message and what tone and word selection do we choose to deliver it? What is the real intention of any given conversation? Let's be conscious and compassionate in how we speak to others and in how we speak to ourselves.
- ❖ Actions – Our days are filled with an infinite number of actions. Can we become mindful of what actions we are taking in any given moment? Can we infuse each action with love, kindness and gratitude? Can we be intentional in our actions? Remember: even when we think they are unnoticed, our actions, and more importantly, the energy we put into them have profound and far-reaching effects. Be very conscious of your actions.
- ❖ Environment – We want to be mindful of creating an environment (and/or being in environments) that support our intentions. While this isn't always possible, creating our

core environment is a powerful first step. On a larger scale, we want to be intentional in terms of how we interact with the environment at large—treating it with care and respect, and in doing so, contributing to its vitality and longevity.

- Being – Living from an intentional place is the essence of really *being*. This is our greatest power and gift. Who do you want to *be* in the world? How does this purpose and meaning *live* through you? This *being* is also a practice. It is a way of living and breathing our essence and having a profound effect on everything and everyone we encounter.
- Nourishing – Any vital being needs nourishment to satiate it and to help it thrive and flourish. Consider how you are nourishing your body, your mind and your spirit. What kind of conditions are you creating for yourself such that your intentional self can truly grow?
- Awareness – Observe what is going on all around you. Take it in through all your senses. Allow all this input to be processed, not just at the level of the mind, but also of the body, heart and spirit. When we are fully aware, we can take in information beyond of our normal patterning and filters. We can listen at a deep level and use this information to respond to the world in a meaningful way.
- Response – Instead of knee-jerk reactions fueled by ego, emotion and our patterning, can we pause? Can we be aware of what's going on around us, take time to let it sink in a little bit, and respond to the world from a heart-centered and intentional place?
- Support network – Take a good look around and ensure you are surrounding yourself with people who support your most intentional life. These could be friends, family, teachers, mentors, coaches, healers—really anyone who has your best interests at heart and supports you from this place. You don't need to discard the others. You just need a strong support network to draw on when life happens (which it will).

And, the cycle begins again. With each integration, we connect deeper to our truest selves, to our purpose and our joy. We can look at what's working and discard what's not. We can also modify as we need to. With deeper connection, comes deeper listening and greater integration. This cycle moves us upward and the chaotic distractions that used to plague us seem to fall away. Because I can't remind you enough, this is a practice that you can have fun with and be curious with. It is meant to cultivate greater joy and freedom. It requires your effort, but remind yourself that you don't need to be so serious. Relax into it and enjoy the fruits of your efforts.

Special Intention Setting Practices

There are times where we feel compelled to reflect, take stock and re-connect with our life's purpose and what we want to create for ourselves. While we can set day-to-day and moment-to-moment intentions, sometimes we want to set intentions that will underpin longer periods of our lives, like years. Milestones provide powerful opportunities to reflect and set intentions.

New Years

The new year is one of my favorite times to take stock and set intentions that will be the creative energy that inspires the coming year.

A beautiful way to mark the new year can be to create a list of what you are grateful for from the previous year. Recognize your accomplishments, special moments, adventures, lessons, milestones and any other significant moments that have left a mark in your heart.

In looking forward to the coming year, look at all aspects of your life and give consideration as to how you want to show up, what you want to create and what you would like to manifest for yourself. These areas of your life may include health, career, home, relationships, travel, financial well-being, personal growth, giving back, spiritual wellbeing, your dreams, play time, the environment, etc. You will make this list your own but what's important is that you identify the key areas of your life and give attention to what intention you want to bring to each area; what you want to nurture, cultivate and grow. You may also have specific goals that you want to set for yourself. When we get specific, we are aligned with the energy of creation. You may also have an overall intention. Some people like to choose a word for the coming year.

Remember that you play by your own rules, so a new year can be the calendar new year of January 1. But, it could be any calendar that you personally follow. It could also be on your birthday or another date or anniversary that's significant to you. You will know which dates feel like they mark the end of a period and the start of a new cycle in your life. We want to mark these new cycles by honoring what's come before, by looking at the road ahead and by setting our attention to what possibilities we want to align with.

Other Significant Milestones & Life Events

There are so many significant life events and shifts that can shake us up or make us want to pause, take stock of our lives and re-consider how we want to move forward.

These can include births, deaths, marriages, divorces, graduations, illnesses, tragedies, new ventures (love, job or other exciting opportunity), loss (love, job, opportunity), adventure or any other significant change.

No matter how unsettling, use these experiences as opportunities to re-connect to who you are in this moment, who you want to be, what lessons you've learned and what you want to create for yourself.

Nature's Rhythms

❖ The New Moon & Significant Astrological Events

The New Moon represents the beginning of the 29-day lunar month. During the New Moon, the moon and sun are in the same Zodiac sign giving us an extra boost of energy. This is a great time to set intentions. You may want to create an intimate ritual that marks the intentions you want to manifest in the coming month. Write them down. Speak them. Meditate on them. Honor them in some way that connects to your heart and mind. Commit to them.

The Full Moon marks the mid-point of the 29-day lunar cycle when the moon is sitting fully opposite the sun and is completely illuminated by it. During this period, energy is heightened and emotions, dreams and mental processes are all amplified. While there can be discomfort, this can be a great time to connect with the amplified energy to connect with gratitude, abundance and possibility. It can also be a powerful period for creativity. Use these powerful times to re-connect with how you are feeling, what is going on in life and where you want to put your creative energies. Many people also use these periods to cleanse and heal.

❖ The Summer & Winter Solstice

In each year, we have solstices: one in June and one in December. The longest day of the year (longest day of sunlight) is the June summer solstice (Northern Hemisphere) and the December summer solstice (Southern Hemisphere). The shortest day of the year (shortest day of sunlight) is the June winter solstice (Southern Hemisphere) and the December winter solstice (Northern Hemisphere). Wherever you are in the world, these times represent light and are an opportunity to celebrate what this means in our lives. What intentions feel authentic at this time of year, at this point in our lives? How is light represented in our hearts, how we live and in what we are radiating into the world?

(Northern Hemisphere) The winter solstice can be a time to light a candle and connect with the duality of light and darkness. It's a beautiful time to sink deeper inward. Can we rest? What do we want to nurture in hibernation? What intentions feel important right now?

(Northern Hemisphere) The summer solstice is a time of light and expansion. It's a time of expansiveness, of being out in the world and of being in full bloom. What intentions do you want to create that connect and amplify this energy?

❖ Spring & Fall Equinox

In each solar year, we have two equinoxes, one in March and one in September. The equinox is where day and night are equal length. In spring, we prepare for rebirth and waking up from winter. In the fall, we let go and move inward preparing for winter and a period of rest. These natural phases are a powerful time to attune ourselves with nature and coordinate our intentions with what these changes represent in the natural world and within our own lives.

If astrological movements speak to you, I invite you to find or follow a knowledgeable astrologer. They can offer insightful explanations on all the celestial movements, including key transits, retrogrades, eclipses, super moons and other significant movements. They'll also explain the meanings of these events and how you can best leverage these energies in your own intentional rituals.

SECTION Three

MY DAILY INTENTIONS

MY DAILY INTENTIONS

These intentions are meant to inspire you to connect with your heart and your deepest sense of being. Notice how they land within you and what feelings come up. They are intended to connect with your rawness and your divine beauty. They are also intended to inspire and empower you to live into them in a meaningful and purposeful way. Please show up in this world—we need your love, kindness and authenticity.

Read through and become familiar with these intentions so you can use them as a daily resource. Keep this book on your bedside table and choose an intention in the morning (either on purpose or at random). I just open some of my favorite books knowing that this trusted companion will always open just where I need it to. May this book also work that magic for you. Some days, you may want or need to manifest something specific. On those days, turn to exactly what your heart needs and move from that place.

Each intention also has a companion affirmation on the adjacent page. "I am" statements are the most powerful statements that we can make to the Universe. Declare your intention, live from this space and open your heart to everything that unfolds. These statements allow you to enter a deeper place of knowing and create opportunities for expansion and great experiences. Open yourself and invite the abundance.

This book is yours to enjoy. Personalize your experience. Make it joyfully and uniquely your own. May it speak to your soul and inspire many intentional days.

Namaste.

I invite abundance

Abundance

Like the world inside the mustard seed, I embrace the abundance available in the tiniest things and the seemingly inconsequential moments. I open my heart and my mind to the vastness of all possibilities. I remind myself that the Universe works in synchronicities and that life is rigged in my favor. I allow all abundance—expected and unexpected—to flow to me. I receive all abundance that comes to me with my arms wide open. In gratitude and reverence, I also give generously, contributing to and honoring my responsibility in the flowing cycle of abundance.

*I am an activist
in my own life*

Activism

I will be an activist in my own life. In big and small ways, I will connect to my sense of purpose. I will rise up and create change. I will love myself. I will nourish myself. I will be kind to myself. I will do this unrelentingly. I will use my voice, my mind and my heart for my greatest good. I will get clear on what feels true and what kind of environment nurtures my growth. I will surround myself with people, places and things that ground me to my purpose and put the wind beneath the wings of my highest dreams. I will crawl, walk, run and fly towards my most beautiful expression of who I am meant to be. I will take action and commit my energy and my endurance to this great pursuit of a life well-lived.

I choose to wake up in my life

Awareness

I choose to wake up in my life. I choose to be conscious and alive. I will be in the present moment and use my exquisite senses to tap into myself and the world around me. There are great truths in this vast interconnectedness. When I'm aware, I can fully experience this moment and all that it offers me. Awareness affords me access to great wisdom and divine intelligence. With access to these gifts, I can make mindful decisions for my next step towards my highest experience and my greatest good. I commit to being fully present and aware. I sit up. I rub my eyes. I stretch my arms and I am grateful to wake up to the gift of this day.

I can't come to the phone right now, I'm busy being

Being

It can be easy for me to get caught up in doing an inexhaustible list of things. But, doesn't life on autopilot, racing from one thing to the next miss the whole point? I pause, close my eyes and breathe. I remember that the beauty is in the being. In this moment, I open my senses and expand my awareness to the fullness of this moment. I tap into what is going on around me and how I'm really feeling. I embrace and invite the magic and magnitude of all of it. I commit to being fully present and an active participant in my own life. I will meet the world in this moment from a place of deep love and reverence. I will savor this moment and know that the most valuable contribution I can make is being raw and authentic—being myself, being right here.

I honor the beauty within me and all around me

Beauty

I close my eyes and feel the beauty within and all around me. It has always been here in this raw and authentic state. Like a diamond, I am a multifaceted and divine entity created by pressure, tension and stress. I do not listen to outside judgements, definitions or demands on my appearance. I know that beauty is in the essence of my being. I access that place tenderly with love and kindness. I have deep gratitude and unlimited acceptance. It is from this core of my being that I radiate myself to the world. My eyes sparkle. I smile. I see beauty in all things—in the goodness and even in the painful parts. I see beauty within me, and I see beauty everywhere.

I feel the fear and do it anyway

Beyond Fear

For those challenges that face me, I will feel the fear and do it anyway. I will muster up all the courage I have to be open, to grow and to experience the full joy of being alive. I will honor the pangs that want to keep me safe. I have heard them and decided to take risks outside my comfort zone because this is where the magic happens. I embrace the fear and the uncertainty and know that going beyond them is not only worth it, but essential. Fear, I look you in the eye and I move forward, because of and in spite of you, out into the land of adventure, greatness and infinite possibilities.

I bless this, too

Bless This, Too

I know deep down that all of life is a brilliant blessing. I choose to see it this way. I bless its rawness, its beauty and its surprises. I bless the people who show up in my life. I bless my body, my mind and my spirit. I bless my experiences and my lessons. I bless the water I drink and the food I eat. All of it—meeting me like a beautifully wild and lush garden. I bless this moment. I bless you and I bless me. I bless the flowers and the seeds. I bless the dirt and the weeds. I bless all of this. And this. I bless this, too.

Today, I bring the sass

Bring the Sass

Today, I am going to smile broadly, give the Universe a wink and bring the sass. I am here. I am confident. I am going to show up in this world and have fun doing it. This life is a wild adventure and I'm going to meet it and infuse it with big dreams and a sparkle in my eye. I will defy the odds. I will be bold. I will stand in my power and light up the room. I will add a little swagger to my saunter and a healthy dose of an *I've got this* attitude. I will embrace my inner sass and bring its wisdom and brazenness, rising up to meet the world in this moment. This is not a dress rehearsal and I'm happy to be here.

I choose

Choice

I choose. In every moment, I choose. I choose what I will say to myself and to others. I choose to show up as the truest, most authentic and beautiful version of myself because I want to, and I can. I choose to be intentional, mindful and conscious. I connect to my personal power and choose to create a life that I love and live on purpose. I choose love. I choose kindness. I choose to laugh. I choose my friends. I choose where I will put my energy. I choose how I will respond to situations and challenges and pain. I choose, in each moment, to connect to my highest self and live in alignment because that's really the only choice. I choose joy. And—I choose again and again and again.

I am committed to my best life

Commitment

I will get really clear on the life I am consciously creating for myself every day. I will commit to its purpose, its beauty and all the things it wants to align with. I honor that stumbling, failing and disappointment will test me. When these defeats tug me down, I will re-align and decide that no matter what befalls me, I will commit to my very best life and align with my highest self. I will brush myself off, loosen the grip of my defeats and persevere. I will use these as opportunities to dig deep and reinforce my commitment. I will commit to loving myself hard and moving forward despite and because of it all.

I am connected

Connection

I am connected to the entire Universe. I am a collection of interconnected atoms vibrating with stardust. I am connected to all that I was, all that I am and all that I will become in this lifetime and all my lifetimes. I am connected to my exquisite senses. I can hear the birds. I can see the sunrise. I can smell the flowers. I can touch my heart and feel it beat. I can taste all the sweetness. I am connected to my intuition and when I get very still I can allow it to gently guide me. I am like a pebble dropping in the placid lake sending ripples in all directions. I savor this connectedness, honoring the impact that I can make and cherishing the support all around me.

I am heart-centered and courageous

Courage

I don't necessarily label myself courageous, I just am. I show up and move forward in the face of challenges, adversity and uncertainty because it feels important. I choose to operate from a place of truth in alignment with my highest self for my greatest good. I feel inspired and empowered to operate from my heart center and take one step at a time because inside me there is a deep sense of knowing. I'm not bold for the sake of it but because love is bold and so are authenticity and truth. I stand in my beliefs and choose to move from this place despite the odds.

I approach the world with curiosity and a sense of wonder

Curiosity

I choose to be curious. I choose to drop all the things I think I know and relinquish my tendency to judge. Instead, I put on my cape of curiosity and swoop in. I look at things from a place of wonder. I'm fascinated. I ask questions. And—I'm open to the answers that come. I really look and listen. Filters dropped. I find that most of the time what I expect does not come to pass and I delight in letting life surprise me. There is magic in curiosity. I am willing to be in the space of "not knowing" and be curious about people, myself and the world around me. I never know what I might discover!

I defy logic

Defying Logic

In moments of confusion and uncertainty, I will remind myself that sometimes things just defy logic. Things look good on paper, but they don't add up. There's a rational argument, and yet my gut doesn't agree. I will trust my deepest sense of knowing. I will remind myself that the Universe is magical and mysterious. There are many things that defy logic. Many different and seemingly conflicting things can be true at the same time, leaving me in some elevated paradox. I find peace in not being able to explain everything. I trust my deepest knowing and my next best step. I honor the illogical and the irrational and embrace it all.

I embody ease

Embodiment

I breathe deeply. I breathe my intention into every cell in my body. I align my physical self, my highest self and my deepest sense of knowing. I nourish my mind, body and spirit. I move through the world with grace, ease and intention. I also engage my senses. I mindfully touch the world from a place of intention. I observe the world with curiosity and wonder. I consciously slow down to listen to all the things being said and to all the things that aren't. I inhale expansiveness. I exhale and allow myself to sink deeper into this experience and this knowing. I relax and engage in my life with ease.

I am enough

Enough

In this moment, I am enough. Enough isn't lack, but it is the fullest expression of myself in this moment. I am good enough. I am smart enough. I am beautiful enough. I am here in this moment as myself and that is enough. The intricacy of this moment is enough. Everything has conspired to bring me to this moment. There is no deficiency. There is no wanting. There is only the opportunity to show up and to savor it—knowing that it is always perfect. Just the right amount. Just what I need if I am willing and open to accept it. Just enough.

I give myself permission to move forward

Forgiveness

I begin the only place I can—within my own heart. I forgive myself for all of it. I love myself and free her from the past. I leave the pain and regret behind me. I also release the other participants. I detach my story from theirs. I bless them and release them. Staying connected to them energetically does not serve me. They will live their stories and I choose to live mine. I collect all the pieces of myself and hold them with deep compassion. I give myself permission to move forward and I let karma take care of the rest (she's pretty powerful, you know). I choose what I will create with the raw material of my life and I choose to create something exquisitely beautiful.

I am free

Freedom

In this moment, I connect to my deepest sense of freedom. I am free. I imagine that I'm flying, and it feels amazing. There are no walls around me. There is nothing confining me or holding me down. For a moment, I step outside the rules, my responsibilities and my commitments and feel the freedom of my heart's deepest knowing and highest truth. I know that I am free to make choices. I am free to be myself. I am free to love and express myself. I soar. I feel the wind beneath my wings and can see my world from a higher perspective. I taste freedom and decide that in some way I will bring this back to my nest.

*I am grateful
for all of it*

Gratitude

In each moment, I choose to be grateful. I am deeply grateful for all of it. I am grateful for the abundance in my life, for the many rich gifts, beings and experiences that I have been graced with. I am also grateful for the losses, the challenges, my shame and the pain. These are my teachers and I am grateful for their lessons and the opportunities for reverence, healing and transformation. I am grateful for the opportunity to be raw, feel deeply and grow. I am grateful for every soul that has touched my experience and bless them for showing up. I am grateful for the beauty that surrounds me. I am grateful for this moment and all the moments that amount to a life fully lived.

I honor my growth

Growth

I know that I'm here to grow through experience. I commit to living life to the fullest. I am willing to feel discomfort because I know growth is always worth it. I may not understand the lesson in the moment, but I am willing to trust and do the next right thing. I will nourish myself and love myself. I will dance with uncertainty. I will remind myself that although staying open may feel risky and vulnerable, my growth is not only worth it, but it depends on it. I am responsible for my freedom. I will trust nature's cycles and divine timing. I will hold the seeds of my future in my heart and love them hard, allowing them to grow and blossom through many seasons.

I honor my feelings

Honoring My Feelings

In this moment, I honor my feelings. They are the rich, raw fabric of my human life. They feel unbearable and make me writhe in my skin. They point me to things I don't want to look at or are so overwhelming that it's hard to know what to do with them. I will try not to label them as good or bad, positive or negative. I won't numb them out. I will accept them as gifts and guides. They are energy and I will let them pass through me. They are all valuable and worthy of my attention. I will let them be expressed. I do not need to hang onto them. I will let them be big and wild and free. In honoring and releasing my feelings, I honor myself and the fullness of this experience. I use them as an opportunity to navigate back into alignment with my true self. Deep down, I know that they're all OK and they make me whole. I deny no part of myself nor my experience. And—if I choose—I know in my heart that these rich emotions have the power to lead me to my greatest peace, joy and purpose.

I am hopeful

Hope

What else is there if there is not hope? Hope is my highest vision for the richest outcome. It fuels me. It unites me with the world. It keeps me tethered and intentional. When I imagine painting a picture of hope, it is bright, vibrant and radiant. It connects me to my ideal eventualities and the very best possibilities. I will keep hope in my heart where it's safe and nourished. I will let it banish worry. I will move forward from this heart-centered place. I will be grateful for this moment. I will take my next intentional step fueled by love and motivated by hope.

I am a powerful creator

I Am a Creator

I am a wild, passionate and colorful creator. I have the power to create my experience. In every moment, I have the opportunity to be actively creating. I have constructed worlds for myself. I can deconstruct them and create new worlds. Nothing is finite. I can create an experience that is kind and loving, that is full of rich moments and people who inspire and support me. I only need to connect with my grandest vision from a heart-centered place and imagine infinite possibilities. I can create in big and small ways all the time. This is a conscious activity that I choose for myself. I delight in creating a beautiful world that feeds my soul.

I am worthy

I Am Worthy

Why would I let someone else define whether I'm acceptable or even lovable? I fall into this trap from time to time, and when I do, I remind myself to come back to me. I remember to be kind to myself, take time for myself and love myself. I am worthy of all of this. I need nourishment, fulfillment and love. I am a divine and magical creature. I am worthy of time, appreciation and respect. I stand in my truth and know that I am deeply worthy of all I want and desire. I meet these needs within myself. I honor my own worthiness and show up in the world from this place. I create space to be still, to listen to my heart, to fill my soul and to be renewed and rejuvenated. I am worthy of great love.

I savor this moment

I Savor

I savor moments, my time here and all my beautiful experiences. I pause and take in each unforgettable moment. I feel all of it with every sense I have. In savoring, I enjoy and bask in the deliciousness that surrounds me. I see the beauty, the rawness and the magic. I allow this energy to seep into my tissues and my bones and my being. I bite into it like a ripe peach. I taste its sweetness and let its juice drip down my face. Life is a rich and glorious adventure; I commit to savoring every last drop of it.

*I give myself
to the flow*

In the Flow

My life is like a river and I choose to embrace its vitality and be in its flow. No more standing on the shore speculating or trying to swim upstream; I give myself to the movement and energy of life. I trust that I am an integral part of the current of life and commit myself to its rushing waters. There is no straight line as I carve out my path, erode the edges and navigate obstacles. Flow is a natural and divine state and I allow myself to just be here in the magic of creation and the energy of life. All rivers flow to one great ocean of love and consciousness.

I open to infinite possibilities

Infinite Possibilities

People have tried to earnestly tell me what is possible and impossible, but I am going to decide for myself. Why would I build walls around my potential? You cannot suppress my imagination or my appetite for adventure. I know that this Universe is limitless and it does not want me to play small. I choose to release all limitations, and open my heart to explore the magic and vastness of infinite possibilities.

I am kind to myself

Kindness

Kindness is a simple super power. It leaves its beautiful imprint on the soul, bestowing it on the generous heart willing to receive it. This is the delicate dance that connects human souls and breaks hearts open. I begin today with a kind word and knowing glance to myself. I am gentle with myself. I love myself. I am patient. I am worthy and I am beautiful. This kindness can be the most challenging and profound. Connected to my deepest kindness, I will be authentically kind to others and to the world around me. This is my divine appreciation for the beauty that surrounds me and everything that touches my heart.

*I trust my
deepest knowing*

Knowing

Lots of people have advice for me. They tell me what I should do, how I should behave, what's acceptable and what rules make them feel comfortable. But alas, I risk their disappointment to take my own road. I will march to the beat of my own drummer. Why? Because I have this beautiful, deep and sacred knowing. This knowing is an indescribable wordlessness. It comes in many forms—sometimes as a gentle whisper, an intuition or a gut instinct. It is subtle yet strong. It's ancient and wise. I listen for this nudging and look for the synchronicities. This knowing is powerful and divine. It comes from a deep love. I will trust and let this knowing be my guide.

Life is rigged in my favor

Life is Rigged in My Favor

I shift my mindset. I imagine that the Universe is winking at me and I am winking back. I believe that this entire experience is rigged in my favor. Each moment is an opportunity for beautiful awareness. Incredible people and experiences walk with me along my path—some briefly, some repeatedly and some for an extended period. They offer me opportunities to learn, grow and evolve. They are all touched with stardust and I can engage with their magic. I can smile and savor. I know that I am divinely supported. I cast aside small thinking, fear and uncertainty. I am willing to trust deeply. I show up from this grounded and inspired place because life is rigged in my favor.

*I am my deepest
and my highest love*

Love

Today I will love myself. I will look in the mirror and stare into those deep, beautiful eyes and say, "I love you." I will love my smile and the goodness of my heart. I will love my kindness and all the beauty I bring into the world. I will love everything that I create and all that I radiate. I will bring the shameful bits out from the shadowy corners and love them too. I will honor my light and darkness and remember that this is what makes me whole. I will love the gifts bestowed upon me and the challenges that allow me to grow. I will love all of it and show up in the most raw and authentic way possible, knowing that I'm beautiful just as I am. I love myself and I am a true expression of love.

I choose to navigate from a place of love

Love vs. Fear

I commit to my heart being open and full of love no matter what. I will not allow fear to constrict me and keep me small. The world will try to force-feed me fear and I close my mouth, choosing love instead—always. I will cultivate love because it is an expansive, powerful force that cannot be reckoned with. I am willing to feel the fear and I summon the courage of love to help me navigate. I tether myself to the beautiful adventures available to me when I let love fuel me. I choose love and light in the face of darkness. I take each step from this bold place because it is intentional and full of possibility. Love opens me and connects me. It reminds me to revere life and my place in it. I feel love from deep within me and I share it because it's just such a beautiful way to be. I choose love over fear because it's worth it.

*I know there is
magic in my life*

Magic

Today, I will believe in magic. I cannot think of anything more delightful to put my heart behind than a universal wink and all those incredible things that are without explanation. I open to all coincidences and synchronicities. I open to the magic of nature that is all around me. I open to the beauty of stardust and possibilities and tricks. I open to all that defies logic and rational thought for something far more interesting and curious. I open to the magic that is in my heart and always working wonders all around me. Life is rigged in my favor and I wink right back. I cast my own spells and create a beautiful life.

I honor all of me

Me, Myself and I

I honor all of me. I honor the lovely bits. I honor all that is beautiful and radiant. I honor all that is strong and courageous. I honor my sadness and my anger. I honor my resentment and my grief. I honor my joker and my jerk. I honor all the pieces that make me whole. I honor the dark and light and love them because they push me to grow, make choices and show up. I will allow these energies to flow through, honoring them as they pass. I will also give credence, time and nourishment to those parts I want to foster. I honor my wholeness and I also intentionally create how it manifests and shows up in the world. I will use the dark and light energy to cultivate compassion and move myself into greater alignment with my highest self.

I create time

Me & Time

Who's in charge here anyway? Am I ruled by schedules, appointments and constant alarm bells? Or, do I remind myself that I am a powerful creator in control of my time and my experience? I can honor my responsibilities and create time for everything that really matters to me. I create space for love, laughter and joy. I remind myself that this moment is a gift and I will show up in the most meaningful way I can—grateful for the time that is afforded to me. I make nourishing my mind, body and spirit a priority. I will honor my time, savoring it and creating beauty in every moment.

I will treat my life as one incredible adventure

My Adventures

I will treat my life as one incredible adventure. Like all heroes, I may, at times, resist the call as I search for all the safer routes and more reasonable actions. Ultimately, I will heed the call to show up because I am committed to this thing called life. I choose to venture into uncertainty because it's worth it. I'm curious and I'm willing to go to great lengths to know great love, happiness and truth. I know this is only available if I show up willing to be brave and curious. I will step up with immense gratitude for all the great experiences and adventures life affords me. I will rise to the occasion and savor each exhilarating moment.

I pause and breathe deeply

My Breath

What a gift it is to be alive on this planet in this very moment! I gently close my eyes and inhale deeply, feeling my belly inflate. I enjoy the round fullness of my tummy and slowly exhale. In these deep, centered breaths, I connect to the world within me. I breathe in vital life-force energy and I exhale stress, tension and all the unnamed things that are not serving me. This breathing reminds me that my body is miraculous. It is a beautiful and resilient timekeeper. It illustrates the life force energy in the cycle of giving and receiving. With each breath, I'm drawn to all that I have in this incredible moment. I inhale it all with gratitude. I remind myself that each breath is an opportunity to begin again.

I am committed to my deepest joy

My Deepest Joy

I believe that joy is at the core of my being. I know the joy I seek is already within me. I commit to it with a lightness and ease that evaporates all barriers. I will create joyful moments with every heartbeat. I will nourish my mind, body and spirit, and know that my joy radiates in a smile, in love, in kind acts and in embracing life's adventures. In difficult times, I still tether to joy through taking the most compassionate next steps forward. While happiness comes in wonderful highs, joy is my deep and soulful undercurrent connecting me to peace, ease, knowing and great content. I honor my most joyful self and commit to sharing her with the world. I am worthy of joy and am committed to living in this state in each moment. Joy is right here.

I grow into my greatness

My Greatness

I'm tired of being good if that means living by other people's expectations of who I should be and what I should do. Instead, I choose to be great by my own definition. I will tune into my deepest heart center and connect with the truths that live there. I will live with conviction from this beautiful and inspired place. I will be raw and authentic and kind. I will be motivated by love and stand my ground. I am committed to being all that I can. I will untether myself from fear and approval. I will be far greater than "good." I will rise and grow into my own greatness.

I listen to my heart

My Heart

I drop my awareness from my busy mind into my heart. I breathe into my chest and feel its expansiveness. In my heart, I keep many important things—my hopes, dreams and highest intentions. It is the epicenter of my vast capacity to love. With its every powerful beat, I commit to a life well-loved and well-lived. I commit to being passionate and soulful. My heart reminds me of the constant rhythm and power of life. My heart also reminds me that it only functions when it is both giving and receiving. I vow not to constrict my heart but to bow to its fullness. I open my heart in service and with gratitude. I have deep faith in love. I bask in it and radiate it. It is my deepest pulse and the heartbeat of each new moment.

*I connect with
my highest self*

My Highest Self

My highest, most divine self is always guiding me. Full of masculine and feminine energy, she nourishes my growth through winks, nudges and intuition. She puts great obstacles in my way again and again giving me every opportunity to transform and bring myself into greater alignment. She has an incredible sense of humor and wants me to care but not take things quite so seriously. She wants me to love myself and be kind. She wants me to be a joyful creator, to show up and live life on purpose. Life is meant to be celebrated and embraced. Each moment is an opportunity to connect to my deepest knowing, my greatest love and my highest experience of myself and of this life.

I am wildly alive

My Wild Spirit

I connect to my wildest, rawest, truest, most beautiful self. Outside any definitions of right-doing and wrong-doing, I boldly walk into Rumi's field where our souls meet and dance. My heart is free here. This place is boundless, and I breathe it in. It is the expansiveness of my true self before the world told me who I should be, what I must do, what "success" looks like, what is acceptable and what I need to do to be lovable. My wild spirit is my deepest truth, my greatest expression and my highest love. It cannot be contained. It defies rules and explanations and logic. I embrace my untamed spirit and unleash her into a world that is meant to be filled with joy and love and laughter. I feel the wind in my hair, lift my gaze to the sky, raise my arms and invite the thunder. I remember how great it feels to be exposed and wildly alive.

I embrace change

Navigating Change

I embrace change. I release resistance and I invite the possibilities uncertainty creates for me. Change can scare me, and I allow myself to feel the fear and do it anyway—because of and despite it all. In the moments where change feels particularly formidable, I will get very still. I will connect with my most peaceful heart and core of truth where I know that everything is already OK because I've got this. I may be in the fog, but I know the sun is still shining somewhere. I dig deep into my faith and my greatest knowing and take the next step forward. My internal compass will guide me. The path may trip me up or be a series of switchback turns, but I am resourceful and will navigate from my heart, pausing to enjoy the view along the way. I invite change. I am willing to endure discomfort to experience this beautiful journey.

I've got this, too

On Tough Days

While they are heart-wrenching and excruciating, I honor the tough days, too. I know that there is raw beauty here and that hard times are part of being fully alive. I am a willing participant on this adventure. Tough days reveal truths if I let them. I can learn a lot about myself, the people in my life and the world around me. They are an opportunity to get down and dirty. They are an opportunity to get crystal clear on what really matters, and with this, my conviction and commitment to my highest self is strengthened just a little bit more. I am drawn back into alignment with how I really want to show up, what I really want and how I want to live. I will pull together the resources that support and nourish me. I will show up. I will do the next right thing. I will be grateful for this because I know it is meant to help me grow. I use the energy of this experience and this day to move me forward.

My heart is open

Open

No matter how vulnerable and raw I might feel, I will not close my heart over anything. I know that I am vital life force energy that needs to flow. I will honor my feelings, my pain and my discomfort. I will heed their lessons and let them go. I will open my heart to love, freedom and infinite possibilities. I allow this to create peace within me. All things become possible and I am an integral part of all things. I stand in my power and truth with great love and reverence for myself and this experience. I am open to all of it. May each experience break me open even further, creating more space in my heart for the love and wonder of being alive.

*I'm wildly imperfect
and I wouldn't have
it any other way*

Perfectly Imperfect

I don't try to be perfect anymore. I'm raw and authentic and show up anyway. I know that nature and creation is wild and imperfect and that's what makes each tree, flower and being uniquely divine. I embrace my imperfections and spend my time dwelling on more important things, like being joyful, savoring the moment and being in complete and utter love with life and all it offers me. I embrace the magic in the mess. Imperfection is so much more interesting, and I like interesting. In honoring my imperfections, I see that everything is perfect just the way it is.

*I press pause and
savor stillness*

Pressing Pause

I find time for stillness, even if it's only for a few minutes. I close my eyes, relax my forehead, unclench my jaw and give my shoulders permission to drop. I inhale deeply into my belly and slowly exhale. I sink into myself and into this moment outside of time. I venture below the chaos of my mind and into the peace in my heart. I sit here and savor all that the quiet has to offer me. It is an escape from the world and a moment that is just as important (if not more) than all of the other moments. In my stillness, I connect with my truest, deepest self. I become aware of how I'm really feeling. I offer myself the gifts of breath, compassion and acceptance. There are quiet stirrings in this wondrous and magical place. I savor stillness because it is a gift to myself. I promise to press pause more often.

*I will live my
life on purpose*

Purpose

I choose to show up intentionally in my life and live on purpose. I know I can create my own experience and impact the world around me. This excites me and inspires me. I will rise to the occasion and show the world what love and light feel like. I will radiate them with the fierce beauty of the sun. I will surrender to my heart and heed its call. Whether it's a specific purpose or showing up in a meaningful way, I will be mindful of my actions and make a conscious impact from an authentic place of deep love, kindness and reverence for all people and experiences.

I travel light

Release

In my backpack of life, I carry only what I need to sustain me on this leg of my journey. I let go of tired stories and belief systems that don't serve me. I relinquish weights and worries. I ease my load and invite adventure. I put my energy into lightness and being here right now. I carry only provisions that support me, fill my heart and give me the courage to move forward. They are what nourish and inspire me. Releasing my grip and letting go means freedom and hope are available to me. I can travel light and be light.

I have deep reverence for my life

Reverence & Grace

It is not lost on me that this moment, this day, this lifetime is a precious gift. I revere its fleeting fragility. I honor the fullness of my experience and am deeply grateful for it. I know that there is something much greater going on, and yet my role is integral. A meaningful glance, a kind word, an act of love—they all reverberate and are like threads in this larger tapestry of constant creation. I acknowledge that there is grace afoot and the Divine is always at work. This world is a magical place and I am in awe of its infinite wonder.

I show up anyway

Showing Up

The bravest, simplest, most worthwhile thing I can do is show up. I may be messy and imperfect, but I'm here. I'm not ready, but I'm here. And that's the only place I can be—here—showing up as my most beautiful, raw and authentic self. I cast aside all of my ideas of what should happen and open to the fullness of this moment and this experience. I stand in my truth and in the curiosity and wonder of all this moment has to offer me. I allow my insecurities to reveal themselves. I give them a wink and decide to show up anyway. I show up because of and despite them. I show up and let the world surprise and delight me.

I celebrate life

So Much to Celebrate

This life is an incredible gift. I choose to savor each moment and express my gratitude every day. I cast my worries and problems aside along with my shoes. I ground my bare feet and raise my hands in a defiant act of thanks. I feel the rhythm of my soul and oh, how I dance! I sing. I create. I love. I drink it all in and share my happiness far and wide. I celebrate each day in big and small ways taking nothing for granted. I am grateful to be at this divine festival. I twirl and beam.

I will do the next right thing

The Next Right Thing

Sometimes my energy is low, and it can be hard to see the big picture. I might feel depleted or discouraged. I remind myself that all action is action—even if it's small. I am gentle with myself. I love myself. I ask myself, What do I need to nourish myself right now? What is the best thing I can do in this moment to align myself with my highest good? I know that I just need to keep putting one foot in front of the other. Each step will carry me purposefully forward. I just need to keep doing the next right thing.

I savor this moment

This Moment

I know that all I have is this moment. This moment is perfect just as it is. It is a gift that I accept with gratitude and I honor it by showing up in my fullness. I release the past. I undo its hooks and let its stories dissolve. I release worry for a future that is entirely unknown. I know that the power of my life is in the energy of this beautiful moment. It is a moment that I will never know again. I live this moment to the fullest. In this moment, I choose to live intentionally. I choose to stand in a place of love and reverence for the sacredness of the now. I allow myself to be fully present and aware. There is so much magic in this breath and I savor its grace.

I honor the truth

Truth

Sometimes the truth and I are at a stand-off. These are times when what I want and desire or what I've been led to believe are at odds with what is. When I get very still and let the chaos of my mind dissolve, I can feel the truth in my heart. This deep knowing is the grounding whisper of my soul. It may be faint, but I can trust it. When I acknowledge these truths, a beautiful clarity rises within me. It feels soft and kind and like a powerful undercurrent all at the same time. Regardless of whether I like the truth or not, it is undeniable, and it is empowering. I will accept it as an ally and use it to empower my steps forward.

I invite uncertainty

Uncertainty

I used to let uncertainty scare me into standing still. I was reluctant to take action without assured outcomes. That is, until I remembered that there is no such thing as certainty. In fact, most of the things I expect don't come to fruition. The Universe continues to surprise and delight me in magical ways. I open my heart to adventure and curiosity and all possible outcomes. I embrace the wonder of uncertainty. When I move forward with intention, I've already created my experience, and what happens next is full of infinite possibilities. I invite the uncertainty.

What if all things are already possible?

What If?

What if I am beautiful? What if I am brave? What if I love myself? What if I'm enough? What if I'm ready? What if I was born ready? What if lifetimes have delivered me to this moment? What if I'm meant to be right here? What if everything is perfect just as it is? What if I'm already at peace and freedom is at hand? What if I am worthy of my wildest dreams and they are blossoming? What if all I need to do is open my heart and invite abundance? What if I am fully supported? What if I just can't do it wrong? What if life is rigged in my favor? What if all things are already possible? What if I believed? Just … what if?

I honor this experience and take the lesson with me

Willing to Fail

I am willing to fail. I am willing to go out on a limb and try because it feels worth it. I am willing to go for it even if the outcome is uncertain and there is no guarantee of "success" (whatever that is). I am willing to fall down and pick myself up because I'm not afraid of getting dirty, bumped or bruised. I know that the journey is part of this wild and amazing adventure. I'm willing to fail because I actually don't believe there's any such thing. The only failure is not taking the lesson. I will learn, grow and endure. I will love, laugh and be transformed. I will be supported. I will arrive at interesting and unexpected places all because I was willing. Failure was never really part of it anyway. There was only fear, but a beautiful evolution was inevitable and better than I ever could have imagined. What actually happens when I fall is that I find my wings.

I honor everything that makes me whole

Wholeness

I am vast. I am light and darkness. I am my proudest moments and my most shameful. I am abundant and I am scarce. I am strong and I am weak. I am brave and I am scared to death. I am the face I put forward to the world and the tears I cry to myself. I honor it all. There is no right or wrong, no good or bad. All of it carries my truth and I will pick up all of the pieces and hold them in my arms, loving them equally. I look into the mirror, into the soul of my eyes and commit to loving her—all of her—no matter what. I am grateful for my entire human experience. I am whole. I recognize all of the pains and joys and sorrows that have brought me to this incredible moment, and they will all carry me forward. There is strength in my wholeness. I can see that now.

 **And so it is.**

WITH GRATITUDE

I am grateful to share this book with you. I always knew I would write a book (hopefully, there are more to come), but I had no idea that this would be it (nor what it would take for me to get here)! Thank you for inviting me into your life and your heart. With all my heart, I wish you many intentional days.

To Maddie & Jack: you two are hilarious and vibrant spirits who bring me immeasurable joy. I love you deeply and I hope life brings you many rich adventures.

To my mom & dad: for being there with me through thick and thin. I love you and am grateful for all of it.

To Anne: my beautiful soul sister in every sense. You are a blessing to me.

To my beautiful friend Stacey, who heard about this book daily. Your love, honesty and friendship are a true gift. I'm grateful to sit on the ledge with you. Thanks for hanging out there with me—always.

To my friend Jackie, who has not only been a great support but has shown up at pivotal times in the creation of this book. I thank you for all of your divine interventions.

To Christine, a great friend and incredible creator, I thank you for taking my idea for the cover illustration and weaving complete magic into it.

To Sarah, Leslie, Natalie and Karla: you are special people who nudged me and created an opportunity for me to share my recovery story when it still kind of terrified me. I appreciate you for seeing me, believing in me and allowing me to be courageous.

To my fellow master coaches who supported me in infinite ways. You are all special to me and helped me bring all of my stories and messages to life. To JVo for your coaxing and insightful questions. And to Martha whose writing feedback took a long time to sink in, but I finally got it!

To Jenn, Kim, May, Priyanka, Sarah: your friendship means so much to me.

To Caroline and Asha: your friendship and energetic support has made all the difference to me.

To everyone I've encountered on my journey. Countless people have touched my heart, encouraged me and let me know I'm not alone. I thank you all.

To Guru Singh and Wayne Dyer for their wisdom in the world. Their books have inspired me and helped me make sense of things. Thank you for your bold voices, your wisdom and your work in the world.

To everyone who has enjoyed the cards, has come to workshops, joined me online, supported my work and shared the cards with their friends, customers, students, etc. You water my flower and keep it blooming.

To you, the reader, for inviting and integrating intentional living into your everyday. We are better together.

I am deeply grateful and wish you all great joy,

Adrienne

ABOUT ADRIENNE

Adrienne is the Founder and Chief Joy Curator at her company May You Know Joy Inc. Her mission is to inspire and empower people to live intentionally and create their lives on purpose. Her recovery showed her that we are all recovering our truest selves every day and are connected by our desire to create meaningful lives. She left a 15+ year career in media to launch her company. She received her Master Life Coaching certification with Martha Beck who also challenged her to share her story in her own authentic way. Her business continues to evolve as she finds new ways to explore intentional living and how we can integrate it into our every day.

Adrienne believes there is raw beauty in us and in all our moments. She invites you to tap into it through her cards, workshops, retreats, books, speaking engagements, on-line communities and especially in your day-to-day intentional living. It's simple, worth it and full of joy—just like life is meant to be.

Learn more about Adrienne's work and join the Intentional Days online community:
www.mayyouknowjoy.com

Follow on social media:
IG: @mayyouknowjoy   Twitter: @mayyouknowjoy
FB: @May You Know Joy   Share your posts with #mayyouknowjoy